The Great
Tomato
Book

THE GREAT
TOMATO
Book

Gary Ibsen

with Joan Nielsen

TEN SPEED PRESS
Berkeley, California

This book is dedicated to my sons Leif, Bjorn, and Abel (healthy spirits every one), who continue to offer themselves fully as they are . . . to make the earth a better home. I'm honored to be in the company of such fine human beings. Stewardship of the earth could not fall into more loving, capable hands.

A Kirsty Melville Book

Ten Speed Press
P.O. Box 7123
Berkeley, California 94707
www.tenspeed.com

Distributed in Australia by Simon and Schuster Australia, in Canada by Ten Speed Press Canada, in New Zealand by Southern Publishers Group, in South Africa by Real Books, in Southeast Asia by Berkeley Books, and in the United Kingdom and Europe by Airlift Books.

Design by Leslie Barry
Cover photo and photo on page 137 by Batista Moon Studio. Photos on pages 18, 46, 47, 63, 70, 87, 101, 103, 115, 121, 134, and 149 by Robert Neimy. Photos on pages x, 20, 32, 68, 69, 70, 71, 99, 105, 113, and 150 by Kelli Uldall. Photos on pages vii, 5, 11, 15, 35, 36, 44, 56, 64, 66, 80, 96, 129, and 138 by Holly Stewart. Photo on title page and all other photos by Gary Ibsen.

Library of Congress Cataloging-in-Publication Data
Ibsen, Gary.
  The great tomato book / Gary Ibsen with Joan Nielsen.
    p.   cm.
  "A Kirsty Melville book"--T.p. verso.
  ISBN 1-58008-048-0 (alk. paper)
  1. Tomatoes. 2. Cookery (Tomatoes) I. Nielsen, Joan.
II. Title.
SB349.I3 1999
641.3'5642--dc21   98-53268
                                                         CIP

First printing, 1999
Printed in Hong Kong
1 2 3 4 5 6 7 8 9 10 — 03 02 01 00 99

Contents

Acknowledgments

"There's nothin' finer in life than true love and a home-grown tomato." —*Gary Ibsen*

First of all I'd like to acknowledge Joan Nielsen for her invaluable assistance. When it came time for me to finally launch myself into writing a book about my experience with growing tomatoes, it was Joan's encouragement, knowledge of food, skills as an author, and willingness to join me (and teach me) in the venture that enabled *The Great Tomato Book* to happen.

In acknowledging my appreciation I return to certain people who have given generously of themselves to me and, in so doing, nurtured my gardener's spirit, supported my inspirations, and brought me to know more of myself: my Aunt Jo, who introduced me to gardening and manifesting dreams; Christine, who loved me well as I grew cabbages and struggled into manhood; Tom Theobald, who has shared much more than the wisdom in wilderness and integrity of friendship, who taught me about our connection and responsibility to the earth; Terrance Glassman, who has shown me the possibility in community and believed in me for thirty years; Colette Cuccia for opening me to the gardening of myself; Bill and Dorothy Dick, who for years provided our community and me with friendliness, farm-fresh eggs, and land to grow tomatoes; Orlando Campisi, who enjoyed his last years sharing the bounty of himself and his garden; Dagma Beth Lacey who, with me, has tilled and planted fertile fields and shared in such wondrous harvests; Robert, Nick, Joe, Jessica, and Jake Hunton for letting me share in their lives; Peter Sealey for his years of friendship and marketing acumen; Joan Dew, who gave up the wildlife of Los Angeles to join me as editor of *Adventures In Dining* magazine and helped

photo on preceding page: *Yellow Pear*

me turn it into an award-winning medium of integrity; John Teixeira, who has shared his land, his generations of experience, and his passion for organic farming; Tony Medeiros and Tom DiMare of The DiMare Company for the opportunity to learn from their years of growing tomatoes for the world's marketplace and their sponsorship of the TomatoFest; the beloved men (and gardeners all) of "Pegasus," Donald Mathews, Tony Tollner, David Martin, Gerard Rose, and Allen Kemmerer; the garden helpers and friends, Elizabeth Smith, Michael Carini, Philadelphia Welz, Nancy Fleming, Sidney Slade, Lynne Nadolski, Betty Hill, Jim Gallivan, Ray and Betty Bergerac, Jim Gregg, and Ginna Bell Bragg; and to Jackie Lyons, Greg Burford, Felice Larmer, Gary and Suzy Rubin, Susan Draper, Linda and Mike Stemmler, and Shelly Schachter for the lessons and loving contribution to the garden of my life.

To the many tomato lovers and friends from the hospitality, agricultural, restaurant, and wine communities who have said "yes" to me for many years and have supported the TomatoFest; the many talented cooks who generously contributed their recipes; the family farms that have provided nourishing food and homegrown heirloom tomatoes to America's neighborhoods; the soil conservationists; and to the people who provided us the legacy of their seeds . . . thank you.

A special thank you to Julia Child for her generosity, good humor, and personal dedication to improving our understanding and experience of food, and for the many enjoyable years of friendship.

An Introduction
to the Tomato

Introduction

Growing tomatoes has been one of my favorite pastimes in my adult life—a hobby that has nourished me personally and been richly rewarding to share with my family and friends.

Like most home gardeners, I used to select the variety of tomatoes I grew based on what commercial seeds were available at the local garden shop. These were usually the most popular hybrid varieties distributed by the nation's largest seed suppliers. I considered myself fortunate if my selection included a couple of early season varieties, two or three beefsteaks, a paste, and a cherry tomato. Life was simple then, if not narrow, considering my limited experience with tomatoes. And then I discovered heirloom tomatoes.

I was introduced to the exciting and flavorful world of heirloom tomatoes by an elderly Portuguese gentleman who, upon retiring, spent most of his last years in his garden. He delighted in generously sharing his harvest with curious neighbors seduced into his bountiful backyard. He patiently impressed upon me the importance of healthy soil and proper nutrients to produce the tastiest of tomatoes and started sending me home with some of his extra seedlings. With names like Costoluto Genovese and Old Flame, these tomatoes date back generations and come from all parts of the world—seeds were handed down from family member to family member because the quality and taste of the fruit were considered precious heirlooms.

And so my passion for growing tomatoes began. Since my growing space was limited, I would plant tomato seedlings anywhere that had adequate sunlight, often along the whole southern exposure of my house. With vines tied to the rain gutters, every window of the house was covered in a tapestry of tomatoes by mid-season. At harvest time I would invite a few friends who shared my passion for the old-fashioned tomato flavors to a "tasting." Many were professional chefs who were equally excited about these rediscovered flavors and explored them with originality in their tomato dishes. And so it began. First with ten guests—then each year thereafter, as the word spread to others in the community, the size of the tasting expanded along with the number of tomato dishes that guests contributed.

I began finding seeds that were considered favorite old varieties from around the world, including Asia, Europe, and many regions throughout the Americas. The tastings grew so large that I decided to share the event with the public. As a charity fund-raiser that I named "TomatoFest," more and more friends, families, and chefs could experience the tasting of heirloom tomatoes and recipes. Through years of producing these wonderful heirloom tomatoes and the immensely popular TomatoFests, one recurring question has haunted me. "Gary, where's the book?" Well, here it is, *The Great Tomato Book*.

Fruit or Vegetable? You Be the Judge

One of the two questions I get asked most often is, "Is the tomato a fruit or a vegetable?" (The other is, "Why don't tomatoes taste like they used to?," which I'll deal with later.) I usually respond with, "What do you like to call it?" I wait for the person to reply, either fruit or vegetable, and answer "You're right." Scientifically speaking, the tomato is a fruit because it develops from a botanical ovary, the enlarged portion of the pistil, which contains the ovules, or egg cells. Legally speaking, it functions as a vegetable because it's generally not served as a dessert and our government can raise revenue with it classified as such while financially protecting our farmers. I'm not kidding.

This is what Supreme Court Associate Justice Horace Gray said in 1893: "Botanically speaking, tomatoes are the fruit of a vine, just as are cucumber, squash, beans and peas. But in the common language of the people, whether sellers or consumers of provisions, all these are vegetables which are grown in kitchen gardens, and . . . are usually served at dinner in, with or after the soup, fish or meats . . . and not, like fruits generally, as dessert."

The classification of tomatoes became an issue for the U.S. Supreme Court following a dispute between John Nix, a tomato importer who claimed the tomato was a fruit, and a U.S. Customs agent at the Port of New York who considered it a vegetable and therefore subject to tariff. Under the Tariff Act of 1883, in a move to protect American farmers from competition, a 10 percent import tax was levied on vegetables while fruits remained duty free.

In spite of Justice Gray's decision, the tomato has found more and more creative and tasty ways to appear in desserts. As testimony to this, you'll find some wonderful recipes for tomato-based desserts in this book (see pages 123–29).

"Why Don't Tomatoes Taste Like They Used To?"

This is the number one question I get asked, whether speaking to an audience or just with a friend outside the post office.

First, let's talk a little about that "used to" bit. If your "used to" is as far back as mine, then you most likely got the tomatoes you still covet from a local market, who in turn got their tomatoes from a family farm not far away. (Close enough anyway that the tomato was picked ripe, or at the most a day or two away from being ready for use.) Or you got the tomatoes directly from a farmer's roadside stand, or even better still, from your

Big Beef

family's garden, picked ripe off the vine.

But things have changed. For many years, distribution has heavily influenced the kind and quality of foods that end up on your table. There's the good and the not-so-good about that. Back when you were only getting great-tasting tomatoes, you were not able to get kiwi fruit in Vermont. In other words, we are no longer restricted to the seasonal foods grown in our own region of the country. Fruits and vegetables can now be shipped from wherever they are in season. Every year that goes by, there seems to be less and less regional identity to our foods. As people in all parts of the country (and the world) have demonstrated their willingness to pay for foods from faraway places, the demand has increased for foods that can make the trip and still look good enough for the customer to buy.

What has happened to the tomato's taste is a perfect example of accommodating the customer. Most of the commercial tomatoes have been hybridized to meet the demands of mechanical harvesting, disease prevention, distribution, and shelf life. Where taste was once the priority, durability, longevity, and a cosmetically attractive appearance now reign. Commercial tomatoes are typically packed for the market and labeled as either "mature green" or "vine-ripened."

Although no legal standard is in place, among growers there is an understanding of the criteria that enable tomatoes to be classified as "vine-ripened": These tomatoes are picked when pink color appears in the fruit, and ethylene gas is not used to ripen fruit. However, it's fairly common for growers to label their tomatoes "vine-ripened," knowing full well they have not met the understood guidelines. After all, with tremendous competition among growers, no interstate or intrastate regulations, and the consumer crying for only "vine-ripened" tomatoes, there's a lot of incentive to sell you what was picked green, gassed, and chilled, with the label "vine-ripened."

So, what happens in that last week or so of a green tomato's life, prior to ripening? The chlorophyll in the dark green fruit begins to break down, turning it to light green, and then to almost white. This is the stage called "mature green," when most commercial tomatoes are picked. If picked at this stage, they will continue ripening. In the next few days, the color will appear, the acid content decrease, the sugar level increase, and the complex flavor components will begin to develop. Unless you have enough sunshine and heat during this stage, you won't get the greatest flavor possible for the variety, regardless of how great the soil and other environmental conditions have been.

It's as simple as this: A tomato that is allowed to ripen on the vine before picking will have that old-fashioned tomatoey taste. In fact, the USDA found that a flavor component in a vine-ripe tomato was up to ten times greater than tomatoes that were picked while they were still green. But you didn't need the USDA to tell you that.

What about the different flavors associated with different colors? Contrary to what many people believe, yellow, orange, and white tomatoes do not necessarily have less acid than red tomatoes. Often, they have a higher sugar content, and this can mask their acidity. It has been determined, however, that acidity level does vary among varieties. In general, I've found certain flavor characteristics most often associated with different colors: The "blacks" have richer, more complex flavors; the greens are surprisingly citrony/lemony; yellows, oranges, and bicoloreds have a mild fruitiness, sometimes tropical; the reds are all over the taste map, from very mild to bursts of classic "old-fashioned" tartness, balanced with a full sweetness.

When you store your freshly picked or vine-ripe tomatoes, avoid putting them in the refrigerator unless they have broken skins, because this will effectively "rob" the tomato of all desirable flavor. The best place for them is in a well-ventilated basket.

Tomato Talk Made Easy

In the family of tomatoes there are open-pollinated varieties and hybrids. A hybrid is produced by crossbreeding a male flower of one pure and distinct variety with a female of a different pure and distinct variety. This can produce a plant that displays the best qualities of both parents and expresses more favorable characteristics than either parent.

My opinions about hybrids are more negative than positive. Everyone who has experience with hybrids has their own opinions. And there are probably many more people who swear by their loyalty to hybrids than to the open-pollinated varieties. After all, for many years hybrids have been distributed widely by major seed suppliers. They've also been the ideal for farmers who, in supplying their markets, know they have to satisfy the consumer who insists that tomatoes be red, round, firm, and blemish free. But it would be an awfully deprived world if hybrid tomatoes were all you could find to eat.

Sure, there are good hybrids. I have my favorites, the top of the list being Lemon Boy, Sun Gold, Big Beef, and Carmello. What I like

most about the hybrids I've experienced is their ability to produce a dependable, abundant crop even under less-than-desirable and erratic weather conditions. Some varieties are even mouth-watering good.

But while hybrids generally have a commercial advantage in getting to the marketplace, in terms of size uniformity and yield, they also have some features that are less attractive for the home gardener. Hybrids are unstable, and the seed produced from a hybrid will most likely not produce a tomato similar to the quality of either of its parents. And because many hybrids have been produced primarily for their uniformity in size, disease resistance, and shipping endurance, their taste is often sacrificed.

Open-pollinated varieties (OPs) have a long tradition of success, some for hundreds of years. They are produced from the seed of the same variety year after year, thereby enabling gardeners to select and reproduce the favorite qualities of that variety (size, taste, color, shape, hardiness, etc.). Seeds from these tomatoes will produce identical fruit to the parent, and after several generations the qualities that were most cherished will be stabilized. (Most seed will become true after three generations. Some varieties may take as long as ten generations to stabilize.) And contrary to what some hybrid devotees might have you believe, open-pollinated varieties also have a proven record for disease resistance. In the long run they are probably on par with the hybrids for their ability to resist many diseases.

There's an uprising of people like me whose favorite tomatoes are the heirloom and open-pollinated varieties. Since 1985, with the help of

Did You Know?

The tomato, *Lycopersicon esculentum,* is a member of the Solanaceae (nightshade) family and was considered poisonous by many people until the mid 1800s.

The tomato is most Americans' primary source of nutrients among fruits and vegetables, because we eat more tomatoes per person than any other fruit or vegetable (except the potato, thanks to french fries).

Although the tomato is a perennial, it is grown as a warm-season annual because it is sensitive to frost.

Some medical research indicates that consuming tomatoes may dramatically decrease the risk of heart disease.

California produces more than 86 percent of the U.S. supply of processing tomatoes and more than 40 percent of the world's supply.

Tomatoes are the most widely used canned vegetable in the United States.

There's almost twice the amount of vitamin C and beta-carotene in a homegrown, vine-ripened tomato as in a commercial market tomato that is picked "mature-green" and gas ripened with ethylene.

The first hybrid tomato, introduced by the W. Atlee Burpee Company in 1945, was the 'Burpee Hybrid.'

Supported (trellised) tomato plants produce higher quality fruit than unsupported plants.

seed preservation organizations like the Seed Savers Exchange and adventurous seed companies like Southern Exposure Seed Exchange, the availability of heirlooms has increased dramatically. Five years ago heirlooms began getting publicity. And in the past two years food magazines and newspapers have been leading the heirloom bandwagon.

According to Carolyn Male, Ph.D., and Craig LeHoullier, respected authorities on heirloom tomatoes, there are four categories of heirloom varieties:

1. COMMERCIAL HEIRLOOM. Open-pollinated varieties introduced prior to 1940.

2. FAMILY HEIRLOOM. Seeds that are passed down from generation to generation. These are varieties that may not have been available through seed catalogs until recently.

3. CREATED HEIRLOOM. The result of deliberately crossing two known parents to create a hybrid. It is then dehybridized, through the next few generations of planting, by selecting out the most desired plant and fruit and eliminating the undesirable characteristics. At the generation (perhaps five or more) where no deviation is apparent in any of the plants or fruits, the new heirloom has been created. *(Note: See the description for Radiator Charlie's Mortgage Lifter in the Glossary of Great Tomatoes. This variety would qualify as an heirloom under all three of the above criteria.)*

4. MYSTERY HEIRLOOM. A product of a natural cross-pollination. *(It is interesting to note that all heirloom varieties are open-pollinated but not all open-pollinated varieties are heirlooms.)*

What's in a Name?

The name for the genus *Lycopersicon*, the botanical group to which the tomato belongs, originated with an ancient Greek physician by the name of Galen. (*Lycopersicon* translates as "wolf peach," but the significance of this is long lost.) By the mid-1500s, Rennaisance herbalists and botanists were over-whelmed with new plants arriving simultaneously from around the world. They classified many of these new plants utilizing descriptions from classical Greek and Roman manuscripts such as Galen's, and made many mistakes along the way. In 1544, Pietro Andrae Matthioli, an Italian herbalist, published the first known European reference to the tomato. He called them "golden apples," *mala aurea* (Latin) or *pomi d'oro* (Italian, still in use today), most likely because the first tomatoes he saw were yellow in color. He classified them with the mandrake plant, which was in turn classified with nightshade

Yellow Ruffled

plants (many of which were toxic). By the way, Matthioli claimed that his golden apples were cooked in the same way as eggplant, another benign member of the nightshade family; fried in oil with salt and pepper—maybe the first fried green tomatoes!

The mandrake was mentioned in the Bible with the Hebrew term *dudaïm*, which translates into English as "love apples" or "love plants." A love potion was made from the roots of the mandrake plant by Rachel and Leah in Genesis. Quite a few ancient civilizations believed the mandrake to have aphrodisiac properties. With the tomato being lumped into the same category as the mandrake and nightshade, with so much background confusion, one can easily see how the roots of tomato myths grew—from aphrodisiac to poisonous.

The First Tomato

Much of the early botanical origin of the tomato is cloudy, with a relatively small number of facts proven. But thanks to culinary historians like Andrew F. Smith, who wrote the definitive book *The Tomato in America* (see Additional Reading, page 146), we are much more enlightened about the tomato's mysterious past.

The first tomato seems to be a native of the Andes region of Peru and Northern Chile. This wild species of the genus *Lycopersicon* ranged from pea-sized to the size of today's cherry tomato. Through unknown means, maybe by Galapagos turtles or indigenous birds, it migrated into Central America, where the plant was domesticated and its fruit used in cooking. The Aztecs utilized the tomato, along with a remotely related plant from the Mexican highlands called the *tomatl* (*Physalis ixocarpa*), a smaller, green fruit with a papery membrane. It is commonly accepted that the word *tomato* originated from the Aztec word *xitomatl*, or large *tomatl*.

The tomato made its European debut following the conquest of Mexico by Hernán Cortés in 1519. The Spanish combined both words to create *tomate*, creating further confusion as to which plant the name referred, the green husk tomato (tomatillo) or the *xitomatl*. As with other desirable fruits and vegetables that the Spanish distributed throughout their empire, they took the tomato to the Caribbean and on to the Philippines. From the Philippines, the tomato then spread into Southeast Asia and eventually the rest of Asia.

Tomatoes flourished in the climate of Spain and Italy. Both countries played a vital role in establishing a future for the tomato. The earliest known cookbook to feature tomatoes in a recipe was published in Naples, Italy, in 1692, according to the culinary historian Rudolf Grewe.

Fifty years following the cultivation of the

tomato in Europe, it was grown in England by barber-surgeon John Gerard. In *Gerard's Herball*, published in 1597, he considered "the whole plant" to be "of rank and stinking savour." Even though he knew the tomato was enjoyed in Spain and Italy, Gerard's censure of the tomato as poisonous often prevailed in Britain and some British North American colonies for almost two hundred years.

Large Pink Bulgarian

The Tomato Comes to America

There were many claimants to the introduction of the tomato into the American colonies: the Spanish into what is now Georgia and the Carolinas, French Huguenot refugees and British colonists into the Carolinas, and migrations of slaves from British West Indies and the Caribbean to Southern plantations.

Tomatoes were being cultivated for the table in the Carolinas by the mid-eighteenth century. In 1774 the first American references to tomatoes appear in *The Gardener's Kalendar for South-Carolina* and *North-Carolina*. By the late 1700s tomatoes were being grown in Georgia. Used in cooking as early as 1780, they became the most common vegetable grown along Florida's central coast by the 1820s. By the early 1800s tomatoes in Alabama were

Tomato Sauce from 1692

Take half a dozen tomatoes that are ripe, and put them to roast in the embers, and when they are scorched, remove the skin diligently, and mince them finely with a knife. Add onions, minced finely, to discretion; hot chili peppers, also minced finely; and thyme in a small amount. After mixing everything together, adjust it with a little salt, oil, and vinegar. It is a very tasty sauce, both for boiled dishes or anything else. —*Antonio Latini, Lo Scalco Alla Moderna, Vol. 1, 1692, trans. Rudolf Grewe*

being used to make ketchup. At the same time, they were being sold in Delaware markets and in Alexandria, Virginia. Thomas Jefferson grew tomatoes in his gardens at Monticello in 1809.

Tomatoes had spread northward, and in 1812 the first known tomato ketchup recipe was published in Pennsylvania. The Botanic Garden in Manhattan grew "Tomatoes or Love Apples" in 1806, and within a decade they were being enjoyed by New Yorkers. A New Jersey farm journal noted tomato plantings from 1829 onwards. They were grown abundantly along the Delaware River Valley by 1830.

They swept up the Mississippi River, being included in many early New Orleans gumbo recipes, and were grown in Ohio at the turn of the nineteenth century. By 1817, in Lexington,

Kentucky, children ate tomatoes fresh off the vine.
Tomatoes grew in southern Illinois in 1829. In
1832, Ladies of the Detroit Free School bottled
and sold tomato ketchup to raise funds.

Tomatoes made the trip with farmers as they
settled the West. The *Wisconsin Farmer* wrote about
the tomato in 1849 and the *Iowa Farmer* in 1853.
Minnesota, Kansas, and Oklahoma soon followed
suit in cultivating and consuming tomatoes.
California and parts of the Southwest had been
introduced to the tomatoes earlier, through the
Spanish missions. Pioneers brought the tomato to
the Pacific Northwest boiled, dried, and coated
with sugar. Missionaries from New England went
to Hawaii with tomatoes and wrote home about
their astounding year-round growth. America had
finally fallen in love with the love apple.

With the advent of safer canning and bottling
practices at the turn of the century, America's love
affair with the tomato in general, and with ketchup
and tomato soup in particular, began in earnest.
These tomato by-products became a powerful influence in furthering the growth of the tomato industry throughout the country. Who would ever have
imagined that the growth of a worldwide
agricultural product had such humble and
hard-earned beginnings.

Sun Gold Cherry

The Healthy Tomato

Only because of the quantity consumed (the average person eats about eighty-five pounds of tomatoes each year) does the tomato rank as high as it does in nutritional value. The highest eight ratings go to broccoli, spinach, brussels sprouts, lima beans, peas, asparagus, artichokes, and cauliflower. According to a survey taken at the University of California at Davis, tomatoes are the thirteenth highest vegetable in vitamin C and

Boxcar Willie

sixteenth in vitamin A, when compared to the most popular vegetables. Some varieties are known to have higher quantities of vitamins A and C than others. (The variety Carorich, for example, has as much as ten times more vitamin A than other tomato varieties. Some cherry tomatoes have as much as five times the quantity of vitamin C.) Tomatoes are also high in calcium and potassium.

A nutrition label for a tomato would look like this: Cholesterol, 0mg; Sodium, 5mg; Total fat, 5g; Protein, 1g; Carbohydrates, 7g. Percent of daily values: Vitamin A, 20%; Calcium, 2%; Vitamin C, 40%; Iron, 2%.

Because the tomato has a fair supply of vitamin A, it also contains beta-carotene, which has been said to contribute to lowering the risk of cancer. Scientists at Cornell University have identified two cancer-fighting substances in tomato: P-courmaric and chlorogenic acids. Recently, *Prevention's Healthy News* said, "First came studies showing that people who ate the most tomato products had less prostate and colon cancer. Now for the first time, we're hearing that tomatoes prevent heart attacks. In Europe, men with the highest tissue levels of lycopene—the compound in tomatoes that may turn out to be the good guy—were only half as likely to suffer heart attacks as men with the lowest levels (*American Journal of Epidemiology*, October 1997)."

In the Garden

Growing in the Garden

There are about 34 million gardening households in America, and of these, 93 percent grow tomatoes. Because of the popularity of home gardening and the abundance of tomato growers, there's an entire industry devoted to assisting tomato growers and a great deal of information is available to them.

Tigerella

I've found that, from experts to novices, tomato growers enjoy helping one another and sharing secrets of great tomato successes. It's part of the joyful gardening experience. If you are a tomato grower, you are not alone! Don't be hesitant to ask the neighbors down the road why their plants look so healthy. Ask the local nursery or garden shop about fertilizers. Just as there seem to be hundreds of surefire ways to catch gophers, there are innumerable secrets and opinions about the right way to grow beautiful tomatoes.

The tomato plant is a wondrous thing: fragile, resilient, temperamental, prolific, and whimsical, all at the same time. Some varieties may need special pampering, while other varieties are tough and determined enough to push up through concrete.

No matter where you live, as long as you have six to seven hours of sunlight daily, you can grow tomatoes that will flourish and produce fruit. It's easy to go from being a gardening rookie to an all-star in your first growing year. You too can enjoy that big, complex, and fruity homegrown flavor that tomato lovers cherish. Whether in gardens, on rooftops, in barrels, along sidewalks, or even on a windowsill, with just a little time, care, and attention (and information) you can realize an abundant and rewarding harvest.

photo on page 18: *San Remo*

So Many Tomatoes, So Little Space

This is an important subject to discuss, because this is where I first got into trouble growing tomatoes: trouble when my backyard garden took over the front yard, side of the yard, and patio; trouble when there became less room for other vegetables that had commanded garden space in prior years; trouble when the hobby of growing tomatoes required me to redesign family vacations around garden duties; and trouble when canning tomatoes and tomato sauce began to look like a cottage industry! All because my passion for great tasting tomatoes was sorely teased by the discovery of new varieties from around the world. For some people it's difficult to refrain from being tempted by a Sear's, L. L. Bean, or Victoria's Secret catalog. For me, it's hard to resist seed catalogs. My excuse is that I must do everything I can to fulfill the rightful destiny of a tomato seed sprouted into seedling and to encourage a healthy plant into an abundant harvest. Yes, you can plant too many tomatoes.

Twelve tomato plants should be enough for the average family of four to eat, cook, can, and give away. If you love tomatoes, I suggest including in your planting at least a couple of reds (a slicer and a beefsteak); a pink, yellow, orange, and bicolored; a couple of pastes; a "black"; a "green"; and a couple of cherry varieties.

Seed Supplier Savvy

Along with my recommendations for commercial seed suppliers, I highly encourage you to become a member of Seed Savers Exchange (SSE), especially if you wish to keep up with what's available in heirloom seeds. This is a nonprofit organization dedicated to the preservation of heirloom seeds. Membership will give you access to more than two thousand heirloom tomato varieties.
(See Seed Sources on page 141.)

I generally look for certain capabilities from a seed supplier when determining where I will obtain my seeds. However, since I often search for hard-to-find varieties and may locate only one supplier of a variety, I first have to find a supplier that even carries the variety I want. If it's a variety that is difficult to obtain elsewhere, I will probably forego some, or all, of the points below. You will quickly develop a list of your own favorite suppliers and determine the criteria most important to you.

Here are some characteristics of an ideal seed supplier:

- Grows their own seed.
- Can suggest adaptability of variety for your specific region.
- Runs germination tests and offers documentation of the tests.
- Provides up-to-date descriptions and historical data about seed varieties offered.
  (In the rush to meet the growing demand for heirlooms to accompany their usual hybrid selection, some seed suppliers are not as conscientious in providing accurate varietal data. I've found the sources I've listed on pages 140–42 to be reliable.)
- Provides approximate seed count to each packet.
- Is competitively priced.
  (Seeds can get expensive. Some suppliers may be much more expensive than others because they provide fewer seeds in each packet.)

I suggest calling seed suppliers a few weeks before you plan to order, to send for seed catalogs, check on availability of seed catalogs, and get on their mailing lists. Also, if there's a cost for the catalogs, you'll want to pay for them early. This will avoid delays that can occur if you contact a supplier during its peak demand for seed. On occasion, I've had to wait several weeks beyond arrival of most catalogs, for the one catalog that would probably generate the bulk of my business. During this waiting period, I'm often tempted to add or substitute varieties not already on my list. The result has been that, almost every year, I've ordered too many seeds! It is wise to review all your catalogs before placing your orders.

Don't be discouraged from trying to grow an open-pollinated variety that has been adapted to a climate different from yours. I've often had surprising success, even in the first season, with varieties that were recommended as best suited to other regions. If a variety doesn't perform well for you in its first season, rather than being discouraged, save the seed and try again the following season. An attractive feature about open-pollinated varieties is their tendency to adapt to environmental conditions and build up additional disease resistance to new regions after three seasons. But this will work only up to a point. If you live on a foggy coastline, or in the northern reaches where the growing season is short and the climate cold, then I encourage you to try the short-season varieties.

Tips for Successful Planting

In deciding the best time to plant your seeds, you must first take into consideration when the ground is most suitable for planting in your region. Then back up six to seven weeks to allow the seedlings to grow to transplanting size. (I live on the coast of Central California, where spring comes earlier than many other regions, so I sow my seeds around the last week of February.)

Since I don't have a greenhouse, I sow my seeds indoors. It's a seasonal ritual. In my favorite flannel nightshirt, in the late evening, I set up the dining room table with seed trays filled with plant mix, seed packets in alphabetical order, stacks of three-inch white plastic markers and a permanent ink pen for labeling, a pencil, and a notepad and fountain pen for making notes. Then, with the fireplace warming the room and a glass of fine red wine poured, I begin the planting season.

Whether you use seed trays (with or without cells) or small peat pots, use a sterilized, artificial plant mix. Don't use real soil because the drainage will not be as good and the soil may carry harmful bacteria. The artificial mixes must be thoroughly moistened before planting your seeds. Soak the mix in a bucket of water until moist, then transfer the moistened mix to another bucket. From that, scoop the mix to the seed trays and tamp it down to get any air out. Always read the information provided on the seed packet and sow more seeds than you actually need. You may not get 100 percent germination (the federal standard for seed packets is 75 percent, but I figure 90 percent) and some of your seedlings may not survive to be transplanted.

After the mix is tamped into each cell of the tray, push small holes (with the point of a pencil) into each cell, drop a seed, and then barely cover the seed. Do several rows of each variety, then skip rows before starting on the next variety, to help keep varieties separated. In each row, put the identifying plastic marker. When finished sowing a tray, lightly tamp the mix covering the seed in each cell, and lightly spray the mix in the tray with water, being careful to not disturb the seeds.

Then put the tray into a loose-fitting clear plastic bag (leaving the end open for air circulation) and put the tray directly under either full spectrum grow lights or white fluorescents, with a little space between the light and the tray. The temperature should be around 75 degrees. When the seeds start coming up, in about four days, remove the plastic bag and lift the lights a little to allow more space above the seedlings. When the seedlings fully emerge, keep them under the light 8 to 10 hours a day. After they grow their first set of true leaves, give them more light (13 to 15 hours a day), with the light no closer than 2 inches from the leaves. If you don't have grow lights, use window light, preferably from a south-facing window. To keep your seedlings from becoming leggy, which is caused by remaining in high temperatures too long, drop the nighttime temperature to below 60 degrees, lightly brush the tops of the leaves with your hands, and turn the trays daily. (Research has found that either a slight wind movement or gently brushing your hand across the leaves a couple minutes a day

Peacevine Cherry

will produce stronger plants. Also, subjecting the seedlings to a gentle chilling by exposing them to a night temperature of 50 to 55 degrees will encourage, or trick, the plant into increasing the number of earlier fruits.)

A weak fertilizer (like a liquid mix of kelp and fish emulsion) should be applied to the seedlings every few days until transplanting outside.

When the seedlings are 2 to 3 inches tall, transplant them to either 4-inch plastic pots, 2-inch peat pots, or 2-inch 6-packs. Depending on the weather, you may just let the seedlings grow in their original cells and transplant them earlier. You probably won't be able to do that in colder climate regions.

If you find that you have dropped three or more seeds into the same hole and this has resulted in multiple seedlings, cut the ones you don't want with small scissors (don't pull them out). I usually leave them alone if there are only two.

Good Taste Starts in the Soil

Although the taste of tomatoes varies among varieties because of their genetics, I've found that the difference in the quality and fullness of taste has much to do with the integrity of the soil.

Each year I give some tomato seedlings to friends. A few times, I've had the opportunity to taste tomatoes from these plants. Some are grown no farther than a half mile away from me, in the same river bottom soil, same weather, same amount of sun, and similar wind protection as my plants. When sampled, my tomatoes had a much bigger, fuller taste with more of that "old-fashioned" tomatoey flavor. Even though this is probably due in part to favoritism (much the same way that people from New Jersey swear that the Jersey tomato tastes better than any other, and people from New Orleans swear that the Creole tomato is the best), I'm sure the difference in flavor was due to soil quality. Good soil produces better tasting food. Anywhere.

I probably spend more of my time working with the soil than any other aspect of growing tomatoes. Healthy soil feels good . . . crumbly to the touch, fragrant smelling, and teeming with microbial life. Although I can appreciate foods that are hydroponically grown, nothing compares to an earth that is rich in life-giving nutrients, and that will always be humankind's preferred medium for growing food. For the intention of maintaining a healthy soil, there is probably no better treatment than periodic applications of organic compost.

Composting is an important means of recycling waste and a valuable addition to the sustenance of a garden. Compost provides the slow-released nutrients that plants require to protect themselves against disease, insects, and the ravages of nature. It improves the organic matter in soil, which ensures adequate oxygen and drainage and acts as a binder to soil particles such as sand and clay. When active, it also warms. If you don't have your own active compost pile going, purchase organic compost from your local nursery or buy one of the many new compost starter kits. Or, go to the library and find a book that will teach you about starting an organic compost (see Additional Reading, pages 145–46).

Since soil condition is crucial to a successful harvest of great-tasting tomatoes, I recommend starting out by taking a simple test of your soil. You can find inexpensive and easy-to-use soil test kits at most garden shops. They will indicate the status of pH, nitrogen, and phosphorus. (Tomato plants do best at a 6.0 to 7.0 pH level.) Many states offer free or low-cost soil testing. Check with your county agricultural extension office.

There are all kinds of soils. I've found heavy clay soil the most challenging to modify. If you already have deep, loose, and fertile soil loaded with organic matter, then you are way ahead. If you have predominantly sandy or clay soil, you should plan to amend this with enough organic matter to physically alter the composition of the total area you plan to plant. Roughly one third of the soil mix should be organic matter, which can be composed of compost, manure, peat moss, etc. Additional amendments can also be added. (See Favorite Soil Amendments and Organic Fertilizers on pages 39–40.)

Designing Your Garden

The location you choose to plant your tomatoes is important since plants respond best to full sun throughout the day, organically rich soil, water availability, and good protection from the wind.

When my gardens literally wrapped around my house, I picked the whole length of the south side for the tomatoes. I wanted to take advantage of the heat reflection off the house and have the plants close to the patio off the kitchen. I dug my holes for the plants 4 feet from the house and 5 feet apart. When the plants grew to about 3 feet tall, I pruned them and wound plant tie from the base of each stem and upward until I ran out of plant. I continued up toward the sky and wrapped the plant tie to a hook on the overhanging edge of the roof. By mid-season, all the south-facing windows of the house were covered with different-colored tomatoes. Outside the children's room I had planted different-colored cherry varieties. From the inside, they looked like jewels that glowed in the morning sun.

In planning that perfect spot, stay away from northern slopes and areas exposed to the wind. If you live in frost-prone regions keep out of low-lying spots where the cold is most apt to settle. The opposite is true for the hotter regions where you want the cooler northern slopes.

Planting in raised beds can be ideal for small gardens. The soil in raised beds can be easily maintained with broken down organic material and kept loose (almost fluffy). This will encourage better yields from your plants.

Planting the Seedlings

If you are purchasing your seedlings, versus planting from seed, select only the stocky (rather than tall and lanky) plants that are dark green and free of leaf spots and bugs.

Make sure you have hardened-off your plants grown from seed before transplanting them into the garden. Seedlings purchased from the store don't need hardening. Start hardening your seedlings a week or so before transplanting them outside. Begin by taking your plants out on warm days for 1 to 2 hours. Set them in the shade at first. Then, over the next few days, work them into direct sunlight and gentle air movement. Then extend the amount of time they are left outside. After four days, you should be able to leave them out day and night, unless you get a threatening cold snap at night.

When the temperature of the air and the ground are dependably warm, the plants can go in the ground. If you are using row covers, or other plant protection or season extenders, the plants can go out earlier. (I like using row covers when putting them out even when the temperature warms. It offers the fragile seedling additional protection from strong winds, softens sudden temperature changes, and protects the plant from low-flying insects during this vulnerable period.)

Determinates (or bush types) can be planted 2 feet apart. For indeterminates (plants that grow throughout the season, until the cold stops them), which need more space, I recommend 30 inches in between plants in the same row. If you are planning larger plantings in rows, then space your rows 5 to 6 feet apart.

Transplanting is best done on an overcast day or when the sun is lower, earlier or later in the day. Water the seedlings thoroughly about an hour before planting. If you are going to use a black plastic ground cover down the length of the row, this is the time to put it down. Then cut an X in the plastic over the hole. A ground cover is a good deterrent to weeds and serves to warm the soil. It also helps hold moisture in the ground and evens out the water fluctuation to the plant. The only reason you might not want to use plastic is if you live in an area with lots of gopher activity. When the ground is covered with black plastic, you're less apt to notice a gopher problem until after you lose a plant.

Dig your hole about 8 inches deep and 10 inches wide. A good guideline is to make your hole 2 inches deeper than the length of the seedling you are planting, from the base to the first set of leaves.

I'd like to offer a couple of suggestions on what to put in the hole. The first suggestion is the simplest. It will provide adequate nutrition for your plant and will not involve seeking any hard-to-find soil amendments. The second is what I do. It will involve some planning ahead to obtain these organic amendments.

1. Fill the hole one-third full with topsoil you took out of the hole. Add 1 to 2 trowels of organic compost and either some crushed eggshells (for extra calcium), a handful of bonemeal, or a commercial fertilizer that is high in phosphorus and low in nitrogen (such as 5-10-10).

2. Fill the hole one-third full with topsoil you took out of the hole. Add 2 trowels of organic compost, 1 trowel each of azomite, soft rock phosphate, and worm castings, and one half trowel of cottonseed meal.

Next, mix the soil and amendments. Place the plant in the hole up to its first set of leaves. The part of the stem you bury will develop roots. Tall and leggy plants should be buried deeper. If necessary, bend the plant and lay it in on its side, with its first set of healthy leaves just above the soil. Fill in the hole with topsoil almost to the top, leaving a slight well to hold water. Press the soil around the plant and water lightly to settle the soil and remove air pockets. You can use a weak solution of kelp extract and fish emulsion for this watering, which will stimulate root growth for added stress resistance.

At this point, slip a cardboard tube over the plant (from a paper towel or toilet paper roll) or a cardboard milk carton that is cut open at both ends. Sink the cardboard into the soil about ½-inch. This will stop any cutworm activity and give the plant extra protection from the wind. The plant will grow out of this cardboard shortly.

A Crash Course on Trellising

It's easy to wax poetic about trellising: "Weaving the dawn to the dusk . . . weaving the memories and days together . . . threading green tendrils to blue sky, to the fading calls of Canada geese flying toward sunset. . ." Often there are days like this, where there are no other sounds but the geese and the humming of some tunes to myself. Almost in cadence, I bend for another stem, lift and tie it to the crossbar overhead, and return for another. There have been so many uninterrupted hours of trellising tomatoes that my arms and hands know, all on their own, how to move through forests of tomato vines, but sometimes I drive by my neighbor's farm on the Carmel River, see his fields of tomatoes sprawled comfortably on the ground, and wonder why I still choose the seemingly endless mid-summer's task of trellising my tomato plants.

Using the "stringing up" method, rows of tomatoes are dressed with balloons for the TomatoFest.

One of the primary reasons to trellis is that tomato plants respond best to being supported up off the ground so the leaves are exposed to more sunlight and the fruits don't come in contact with soil-borne diseases and ground pests. By trellising plants you can make maximum use of precious and sparsely available land and even gain a one- to two-week jump on the harvest.

Since I almost exclusively grow indeterminate (plants that grow throughout the season, until the cold stops them) varieties, rather than determinate (bush type) varieties, almost everything I grow must be trellised. Needless to say, I have incentive to find a method of trellising that provides the best support to the tomato plants, provides the easiest harvesting, holds the most amount of weight, uses the fewest materials, costs the least, is fully or partially reusable, and still looks good.

I've found several methods of trellising effective for my tomatoes: single stake, wire cage, wire or wood trellis, basket weave, and stringing up. All these methods are for the taller indeterminate plants but can also be adapted to the determinate varieties. Here are three common guidelines that pertain to any one of the methods:

1. If any stakes must be driven into the ground close to a tomato plant, do this while the root system hasn't yet developed to avoid damaging the plant. The best time to set stakes is when transplanting.

2. Tie the stems of the plant closely enough to support it but loosely enough to allow for growth.

3. Be regularly attentive to the plant's growth. Don't let the stems' growth get too far ahead of you. Trying to catch up when the plant is heavy with foliage and fruit will be an arduous task and may cause the plant damage.

SINGLE STAKE. This is the simplest method. Pound a 6-foot long, 2 by 2-foot wooden stake well into the ground beside each plant and tie a couple of selected stems to the stake. The plant may yield fewer tomatoes using this method, because pruning the other stems will be necessary. The wooden stakes can be saved for use from year to year.

WIRE CAGE. This system has been proven effective for indeterminate plants, and the cage will last for several years. Create a wire cage 5 feet tall by 24 inches in diameter, using 6-inch wire mesh. Stand the wire cylinder on end over the centered seedling. Drive one or two 6-foot stakes into the ground on the perimeter of the cage and tie them to it.

WIRE OR WOOD TRELLIS. In a single line, drive several 6-foot stakes into the ground and to them tie 8-foot sections of heavy-gauge, 6-inch wire. Stems can be tied to the trellis or you can weave the stems back and forth through the grids. Wood trellising or nylon netting can also be used.

BASKET WEAVE. This is a good method for tying up many plants in a row, and it's used by most commercial growers. Drive 8-foot stakes 2 feet into the ground, approximately every 6 feet, with 3 plants in between each stake. Once the plants are around 18 inches tall, tie either a heavy-duty natural-fiber line or nylon line 12 inches from the ground on one of the end posts. Then run the line to the next post (at the same height on the same side of the plants), looping the line around the post to secure it. Then go on to the remaining posts until you reach the end. Tie the line to the end post and start back along the row on the other side of the plants, looping around each post as before and keeping the line the same height from the ground. Add new lines for every 10 inches of growth. Boxes of line available from agricultural supply houses make the job considerably easier.

STRINGING UP. If I have fewer than fifty plants, this is my preferred method of trellising. However, it is the most labor intensive. You can set this trellising system up in a single line of multiple 8-foot sections, or just one section positioned in one or more locations. Unlike the other trellising methods, this will have to be constructed *before* you set in your transplants. Into two 8-foot-long, 2-by-2 posts, drill a 2-inch hole in one end (to accommodate a long nail that will hold your crosspiece). Hammer flat 2 inches of each end of an 8-foot-long, ¾-inch-diameter electrical conduit pipe. About ½-inch from each flattened end of the pipe, drill a nail hole the same size as you drilled in the ends of the posts. Dig two 1½-foot holes along the row where you will plant, exactly 8 feet apart. Set the posts into the ground with the holed ends up. Before the posts are fully vertical, attach the conduit to the top of each post by slipping a nail through the hole of the conduit and into the post (you should be able to pull the nail out with your fingers). Stand each post up, level them to the same height, fill in each hole, and pack the soil around each post. The horizontal conduit should be level and the posts vertical (using a level is easier than eyeballing it). Until you get a feel for doing this alone, it will probably take two people. The horizontal conduit can support more weight (when the plants are full of fruit) than a wire or 2-by-2 wood crosspiece, and you can use it every year. When your plant is around 2 feet tall, tie the loose end of a line of plant tie to the base of a main stem, wind the plant tie around the stem to the top of the plant, then take the line over the overhead bar and tie it off. As the plant grows, untie the line and wind it farther up the plant, pull it snugly to hold the plant up, and tie it off again. Do the same for 3 to 4 main stems per plant. (I've found the best plant tie for this is Grant's Plant Tie that comes in a can. You weave the can around the stem while the tie is being released from the can. The tie is made of a thin, paper-covered wire that holds weight well and breaks down after the season.)

"Stringing up" tomato by winding plant tie around stem

The Fine Art of Watering

For years I preferred watering my plants with a watering can or hose. This process slowed me pleasurably down. It gave me opportunity to pay attention to what was happening with each plant. I got a great deal of pleasure from watering the garden at the end of a busy day. When I increased the quantity of plants to much larger numbers, however, it became impractical as well as a

*Using "stringing up"
method, tie each stem
over crossbar.*

disservice to the plants, because my watering schedule became erratic. I use a drip system now. And the water is on a timer so I can be sure that the plants get the amount of water they need on schedule. If you water by hand, be careful to avoid splattering plants' leaves with mud as this may contribute to disease problems.

How frequently you water depends on the climate you live in and what stage of growth your plant is in. If your soil is sandy, shallow, or both, watering twice a week may be necessary. If you have deep soil where the roots are able to reach down into the soil, you may need to water deeply only once a week. In a heavier soil you should water as infrequently as the plant would like. (The plant will let you know. If it looks droopy at the end of a hot summer's day, don't be too concerned. It may recover during the night. If it still looks wilted in the morning, then water it.) It's important to make sure you don't keep the soil saturated to the point where there's no room for air in the soil.

Keep your tomato plants regularly watered during the season, particularly during dry periods. If the plants are subjected to dry spells, their growth rate will slow down and the fruit may crack when it is watered again and swells. The plant survives by absorbing water-carrying dissolved nutrients. If the plant goes dry, it is more vulnerable to diseases like blossom end rot, a leathery blackening of the fruit on the blossom end that happens when the plant is unable to absorb calcium. Using a mulch of plastic, straw, or even grass clippings will even out the wet-dry surges and slow down the rate of the soil's evaporation.

Not to be ignored are the cycles of the plant's life that instruct you to give it more or less water. You will need to water more often when the tomato plant is very young. As the plant develops, you should water less often but for longer periods to encourage the fine roots to reach deeper. A deeper root system will help even out the fluctuations in moisture your plant may be subjected to.

What to Feed Your Tomatoes

I'm sure there are many gardeners who are blessed with good soil year after year and don't need to add any fertilizer to their tomato plants. The only person I know of who's this lucky tends to his soil by growing off-season cover crops. Then he turns them into the soil each spring to nourish and maintain a desired level of organic matter. However, even though I practice similar treatments to the soil, I believe that feeding tomato plants while they are growing produces healthier, more disease-resistant plants, with better-tasting, more nutritious fruit.

Tomatoes are heavy feeders. Although I sometimes add fertilizer to the ground water or side-dress the plants, I always feed the seedlings, amend the soil before planting, and foliar feed the tomato plants several times during their growth.

Foliar feeding addresses the more immediate needs of a plant versus the long-term and slower method of ground feeding. All plants absorb nutrients through their leaves and stems in addition to their roots. They absorb foliar sprays almost twenty times faster than soil-applied nutrients. (This is kind of like the difference between eating and digesting a meal versus receiving an IV.) Foliar feeding can also compensate for deficiencies in the soil, fortify the plant in the midst of stressful weather conditions, and be timed to enhance the plant's growth at critical cycles. If you wish to add foliar feeding to your plants, you can find assistance and products from companies like Gardens Alive! and Peaceful Valley Farm Supply (see pages 142–43). Foliar feed your tomatoes every two weeks with a weak application of a mix (primarily consisting of fish powder, kelp, microbial digested bone meal, and trace minerals) early or late in the day when the leaf pores are open.

If you use a commercial fertilizer, don't try to outguess the manufacturer. Follow directions closely. It's not difficult to damage your tomato plant. I've included a list of some of my favorite organic fertilizers (see Favorite Soil Amendments and Organic Fertilizers on pages 39–40). I may use some or many of these during the plant's life, but almost any commercially available fertilizer near a 5-10-10 should work well for you. If you choose to start your plant without adding fertilizer, pay close attention for indications that the plant might require feeding (yellow foliage, slow or stunted growth, etc.). On the other hand, too much of a good thing is still too much. If you give your tomatoes an excessive amount of nitrogen, the plants will produce lots of lush leaf growth at the expense of the fruit. Use your best judgment.

*A tomato tasting set up in a
125-foot-long tomato arbor*

Favorite Soil Amendments and Organic Fertilizers

Over the years, I've gradually moved away from using commercial fertilizers, which are the most readily available. Not so much because they don't work (many work very well), but because I've found that I have more control over the quality and specific purpose of each fertilizing amendment I use. Through comparative tastings, I've found my tomatoes have a bigger, more distinctive tomatoey taste, besides being more resistant to stress and insects, since I started carefully selecting the soil and foliar fertilizers I apply. Here are some of my favorites.

AZOMITE. This natural fertilizer is actually an ancient aluminum silicate clay mixed with many marine minerals. It has been used for more than fifty years as a source of many trace minerals. I swear by it. Mix into soil prior to planting.

COMPOST. Whether you use your own or purchase it, this is a primary source of providing organic matter and restoring microbial life to the soil. Apply to soil prior to planting.

COTTONSEED MEAL (pesticide free). This is used as an all-around source of slow-release nutrients. Apply to soil prior to planting.

FISH POWDER. This is heat-dried fish material turned into a water-soluble powder and an excellent source of nitrogen, phosphorus, and potassium (NPK). Apply in ground watering or through foliar fertilizing (combined with kelp extract).

GYPSUM. This is used to moderate (lower) pH, add sulfur and calcium, and loosen clay soils. Apply to soil prior to planting.

LIMESTONE. This is used to raise pH in acidic soils and to correct calcium deficiencies. May be applied to soil before planting, in ground watering or through foliar feeding, because it is compatible with other foliar fertilizers.

KELP EXTRACT. This contains potent concentrations of trace minerals, amino acids, micronutrients, and vitamins that stimulate cell division and root development. Kelp is used not only as a growth stimulant but also for increasing crop yields and for stress recovery. Can be used in ground watering or applied as a foliar fertilizer (combined with fish powder).

SOFT ROCK PHOSPHATE (also called colloidal phosphate). This is the best natural source of phosphorus and calcium. Different from the hard phosphate sold by most nurseries, soft phosphate is an immediate and long-term source of phosphorous. Apply to soil prior to planting.

WORM CASTINGS. This is used for humus and all-around fertilizing. Use a mix that is almost pure castings with little soil included. Apply to soil prior to planting.

Note: Any commercially available, slow-release (granular) fertilizer that is high in mineral content and contains no weed seeds or environmentally unsafe materials is also perfectly suitable.

Saving Your Tomato Seeds

The seeds from your open-pollinated tomatoes are the link to tomatoes that may reach back hundreds of years from many corners of the world. Two generations ago it was a necessity to choose the best plants for saving seed. This assured a good crop for the following years. Today's gardeners are fortunate to have an abundance of open-pollinated varieties to choose from courtesy of the immigrants who settled this country. They brought with them the seeds they cherished, often smuggled in, hidden in clothing and other possessions.

As farms disappear and townships become less rural, countless varieties of heirlooms will have difficulty finding new gardens to grow in. Some are probably still unknown outside the rural farm towns where gardeners have maintained their seed strains. Few of these family heirloom varieties have made it to seed suppliers for distribution. Even if they did, the chance of the seed reaching today's gardener is lessened each year. From 1984 to 1988 almost a quarter of all the small seed companies in the U.S. and Canada went out of business or were bought up by large corporations that replaced regionally oriented, open-pollinated varieties with hybrids that would attract a larger market. Varieties are being lost at such a rate that it's possible that many of the best open-pollinated varieties available now will not be available in the near future. Saving seeds is not only the best way, but probably the only way to be assured of planting your favorite heirlooms in the future. I must offer a pleasant warning here. For as easy as it is to become passionate over growing and enjoying the taste of tomatoes, it's just as easy to become captured with seed saving.

The seeds you collect to save should be from open-pollinated varieties planted at least ten feet away from other varieties. Otherwise, you may get crossbreeding due to wind, bee pollination, or other environmental variables. For cherry tomatoes, twenty-five feet is recommended. Natural cross-pollination (NCP) occurs frequently if two different varieties are planted too close to one another. (I've had some pretty interesting fruit that resulted from this, although the results were nothing I was able to identify or wished to grow deliberately.)

Save seed from your healthiest plants. Pick fruit from several vines. Pick a variety of fruit sizes, not just your biggest ones. If you've been a bit greedy and eaten up all your perfectly ripe fruit, use fruit that has become overripe. Even those tomatoes that have fallen to the ground (and remained intact) should be all right, because the fermentation process will eliminate any bacteria and viruses, leaving you with clean seed. Be prepared. Going through the cleaning of seeds after fermentation is a messy, smelly job but worth getting used to. Most people quickly create a technique that works best for them. My own method has been modified several times as I constantly learn from experience shared by others.

Cut open the tomato and squeeze the pulp and seeds (not the skin) into a clear plastic container (the kind you find in a deli) or a glass jar. Label with the variety name. The container should be one-half to three-quarters full. Don't mix, because that may introduce oxygen, which is a deterrent to the fermentation process. Make sure you don't mix up any of the fruit with your next variety to be squeezed. Clean your hands off in between varieties. Allow the containers to stand at room temperature or, ideally, outside in the shade where they won't be disturbed. After four or five days a fungus will have developed on the surface and most of the seeds will have dropped to the bottom. Scrape off the layer of pulp with the fungus into the trash. Don't worry about the loss of a few seeds still attached to this layer. You may then pour the balance into a sieve and run it under tap water until there are only clean seeds left. Or you can try a method passed onto me by Dr. Carolyn Male. Sit outside with a bucket between your legs to collect the pulp and fungus you pour off. With a garden hose in one hand, spray some water into the remaining pulp mix in the container. The good seeds will sink and you can pour off the floating debris. Do this again several times, until there are only seeds on the bottom and clear water. (Kind of like panning for gold, but easier.) Pour off the water and spill the seeds onto a paper plate or coffee filter that you've labeled with the variety name ahead of time. Thin the seeds so they are in a single layer and not piled on top of one another. Allow them to dry thoroughly. If they remain damp they may germinate. When dry, put the seeds into a labeled envelope and put the envelope in a closed jar, or put the seeds directly into a screw top vial and label with the variety name and year. Store the jars in a cool, dark place. Your seeds should keep for several years.

German Red Strawberry

A Glossary of Great Tomatoes

Some Recommended Favorites

This chapter is a list of my favorite tomato varieties, separated into categories and listed by their varietal names. I've attempted to provide as much useful and historical information as I could for each one. However, for many of the varieties listed, there was little or no information available about their origins. In these instances, I deferred to physical descriptions of the plants and fruit, with comments from my tasting notes for eating and cooking purposes.

Most of these are heirloom varieties. Some of them may have been rediscovered only recently, after having been lost, forgotten, or unavailable for many years. I've also included my favorite

Dona

Brandywine

Mandarin Cross

Carmello

Yellow Brandywine

Amish Gold

hybrids because of their great taste and other qualities that distinguish them above most of their hybrid peers.

Within this selection, you will find some cooler weather varieties most suitable for shorter growing seasons and coastal or foggy/overcast regions. There are also varieties most suited for hotter weather and longer growing seasons. When shopping this list for choices to include in your own garden, consider trying a couple from each of the categories in different sizes and shapes. This will provide you with a tasty and colorful selection. Seeds for most, if not all, varieties listed can be attained through the seed companies I've suggested in this book (see Seed Sources, page 140). All varieties are open-pollinated indeterminates unless indicated otherwise.

Yellow Stuffer

Winsall

Marmande

Big Beef

Lemon Boy

Tigerella

Purple Calabash

Yellow Pear

Green Grape

Sun Gold

Cherry Tomatoes

AUNT RUBY'S YELLOW CHERRY. Yellow, round 1-inch cherry; very productive; fruity, tart flavor.

CHADWICK. Named after the late master gardener Alan Chadwick, originator of the biointensive method of gardening. Flavorful 1-inch, red fruits borne in vigorous clusters of six.

GOLDEN PEARL. This heirloom bears gold-colored, thumbnail-sized pearl tomatoes. Fruits borne in luscious grapelike clusters. Beautifully displayed on a salad or elegantly dress many foods.

GREEN GRAPE. This compact heirloom was developed only a few years ago. Its fruits have become popular in restaurants and markets because of their unique attractiveness and flavor. The 1- by 1½-inch ripe fruits are yellow-green with a translucent pale green on one end, resembling large grapes. A taste and visual treat for your garden. Semideterminate.

ISIS CANDY CHERRY. This new variety produces a delightful, 1-inch round, yellow-gold cherry with red marbling. The delicious taste is rich and fruity.

Isis Candy Cherry

Peacevine Cherry

PEACEVINE CHERRY. This tomato is named because of the high amino acid content, which has a calming effect on the body. According to Seeds of Change, this variety had "the highest vitamin C content in a cherry tomato among 30 varieties analyzed by Rutgers University." One-half-inch to ¾-inch red fruits grow in tresses and have a wonderfully intense flavor.

PINK PING PONG. Produces amazing yields of sweet pink fruits the size of Ping-Pong balls. Juicy and bursting with superb flavors. Great for salads, canned, or popped in your mouth off the vine.

PRIZE OF THE TRIALS. "Rated best overall for flavor, yield, and crack resistance of all cherry tomatoes" in Seeds of Change trials, this bears an abundance of apricot-sized orange fruits that seem to glow.

RED CURRANT. Thought to be related to the wild red currant of South America, the original tomato. Tall vines yield an abundance of rich tasting, tiny, round, ½-inch fruits in clusters of 12 or more, not all ripening at the same time.

Riesentraube

RIESENTRAUBE. This is an heirloom originally from East Germany that is said to have been grown by the Pennsylvania Dutch as early as 1856. From large sprays of flowers grow flavorful red, 1¼-inch fruits that are pear shaped with a pointed end. They grow in generous clusters of 25 to 40, and their name translated from German means "giant bunch of grapes."

ROSE QUARTZ. These deep rosy-pink hybrid fruits are a Japanese specialty and widely marketed throughout Asia, where their elegant pink color is preferred. The plant bears big clusters of fruits with a high sugar content throughout the summer season. Another favorite for a great salad mix.

RUBY PEARL. Beautiful grape-sized ruby-red fruit are borne from this Chinese hybrid. Tall vines bear loads of easy-to-harvest clusters of 16 or more jewel-like tomatoes. This variety is known to grow easily in most climates. Great for garnish, snack, or salads.

Snow White

SNOW WHITE. This hybrid bears beautiful ivory-colored ½-inch fruits that ripen to pale yellow and are so deliciously sweet (without being sugary) that it is difficult to keep from snacking on them. A real child pleaser.

SUN GOLD. A Japanese hybrid that bears rich tasting cherry tomatoes with an intense golden-orange (tangerine) color that literally glows on the vines. Three-quarter-inch fruits are borne on long tresses all season so you'll have hundreds of jewel-toned fruit of exceptional sweetness and quality. Balanced, intense flavor and colorful appeal make this a personal favorite to grow every year.

SWEET 100 PLUS. Splendid hybrid bearing heavy clusters of bright cherry-red ¾-inch fruit all summer. This variety is more crack resistant, with a more balanced, tomatoey flavor than the original and popular Sweet 100.

YELLOW PEAR. This prolific heirloom, first grown in the late 1800s, is one of today's most popular cherry tomatoes. The 2-inch pear-shaped cherry tomatoes are clear sunny-yellow, low in acid, and delightfully sweet. A tasty and decorative addition to any salad.

Red Tomatoes

ANDREW RAHART'S JUMBO RED. This New York heirloom beefsteak, passed down from Andrew through his son John, bears 12- to 16 ounce fruit with intensely red skin and flesh. This is the kind of delicious, juicy tomato to eat over the sink or outside.

Andrew Rahart's Jumbo Red

BIG BEEF. A hybrid that won the '94 All-American Selections Award, this is a splendid version of everybody's old favorite. These giant juicy fruits combine old-fashioned beefsteak flavor with heavy yields. The round to globe-shaped fruit averages 1 pound and its flavor is full and hearty with lots of sweet juice. These giants slice up perfectly for big sandwiches. The fruit stays large even at the end of a long harvest season.

BOXCAR WILLIE. A New Jersey heirloom that produces a heavy yield of 10- to 16-ounce smooth, red, excellent tasting tomatoes that are shaped like globes. Because these are so dependably tasty and abundant, this is a staple in any garden.

BURBANK SLICING. This heirloom was developed by plant authority Luther Burbank around 1914. It produces delicious 6- to 8-ounce red slicing tomatoes. It does well in dry climates. The bushy, prolific plant grows to around 3 feet.

CARMELLO. The French hybrid Carmello is among the most productive tomatoes ever bred. It is popular in European markets because of its exceptionally fine flavor.

Carmello

It bears large crops of heavy, juicy tomatoes with flavor that just doesn't stop, even in cooler weather. Good for slicing in salads, sautéed, or as an integral part of any dish.

COSMONAUT VOLKOV RED. A Ukrainian variety named after the famous Russian cosmonaut who died while landing, Russians grow this for prize-winning fruits. Its round, slightly flattened, 4-inch fruits have a full, complex flavor and nice acid-sweet balance.

COSTOLUTO GENOVESE. This Italian, heat-loving heirloom tomato has been enjoyed for many generations along the Mediterranean. The large deep-red fruits have a singularly fluted profile and are deeply ridged and heavily lobed. They are meaty, full-flavored, slightly tart, and delicious. Because of its scalloped edges, it's perfect for use in an arrangement of different colored sliced tomatoes. It also makes a rich and pungent pasta sauce.

Costoluto Genovese

CREOLE. Developed in Louisiana to excel in the hot, humid climate, this produces heavy harvests of 12-ounce red tomatoes that are firm, juicy, and loaded with old-fashioned tomatoey flavor. Many people, especially those from Louisiana, are religiously loyal to it.

DONA. This excellent hybrid was bred by the French specifically for their customers in markets, where flavor and quality standards are uncompromising. The slightly flattened, almost seedless, round tomato has a sweet-acid balance that few modern tomatoes can match. The heavily producing plants yield 6-ounce juicy fruits that are smooth, meaty, and deep red in hue.

DRUZBA. A Bulgarian heirloom introduced in 1995, this plant produces big harvests of smooth, round, deep-red, juicy 10-ounce fruit. It boasts an excellent, sweet-tart, juicy flavor.

Enchantment

ENCHANTMENT. This "saladette," or egg-shaped, hybrid tomato has been referred to by Shepherd's Garden Seeds as "a gardener's version of Faberge's fabulous jeweled eggs" because of its glossy, red 3-inch ovals that grow in heavy clusters. The fruits have delicate and superior old-tomato flavor, with a well-balanced sugar-to-acid level.

GERMAN RED STRAWBERRY. Introduced by Dr. Caroline Male in 1995, this German heirloom produces large, red, oxheart-shaped tomatoes that are shaped like large strawberries. Plants yield an abundance of meaty, 3-inch-wide by 3½-inch-long fruit that can grow to 1 pound. Although the shape of fruits can be inconsistent, they bear copious amounts of delicious "old-tomato" flavors.

MARMANDE. This French heirloom produces 6- to 8-ounce deep-red fruits that are meaty and lightly lobed with a complex taste. It does well in the cooler summer conditions of California's bay areas as well as hotter regions and is great for slicing or as a stuffing tomato. This tomato is shown on the cover of the book.

OREGON SPRING. This is a popular variety for early silver-dollar sized, bright-red tomatoes.

The earliest fruit have little or no seeds. An indeterminate bush developed at Oregon State University for gardeners with cool summer seasons, the fruit is slightly flattened, sweet, and juicy.

RUSSIAN 117. This oxheart heirloom bears 1- to 2-pound red, heart-shaped fruit that's juicy with solid flesh and an excellent, robust tomato flavor.

RUTGERS. Developed by the Campbell Soup Company in 1928 and improved by Rutgers University in 1943, these compact plants produce 6-ounce red fruits that, for many years, have been considered a reliable crop in the garden. The thicker walls of this determinate lend to its popularity as a great canning tomato.

STUPICE. This heirloom from Czechoslovakia is a cold-tolerant tomato that bears an abundance of sweet, flavorful 2- to 3-inch fruit. A 1988 comparative tasting in the San Francisco area gave it first place for flavor and production.

ZOGOLA. An heirloom beefsteak from Poland, this plant produces luscious 1-pound crimson-red fruit borne from abundant clusters. The tomatoes reach 4 inches across with mild fluting at the shoulders and are very juicy with a balanced and full sweet flavor.

Pink, Black, and Purple Tomatoes

ANNA RUSSIAN. This heirloom oxheart variety handed down to an Oregon woman from several generations within her Russian family is a large, visually beautiful, juicy, pink-red, heart-shaped tomato that normally weighs about 1 pound. It has superb rich flavors. A top favorite juicy pink.

ARKANSAS TRAVELER. Developed for the South by the University of Arkansas, this heirloom is a great hot-weather producer of abundant harvests. The 8-ounce round fruit is flavorful and rose-pink.

AUNT GINNY'S PURPLE. This potato-leaf, beefsteak heirloom bears deep-pink, juicy fruit that weigh 12 to 16 ounces. The flavor is so good that it rivals the Brandywine for excellence.

Aunt Ginny's Purple

BLACK KRIM. The prolific heirloom from the Black Sea of Russia has fruit that is slightly prone to cracking but appealing regardless. The dark, brown-red, 12-ounce fruits are rich and complex in flavor, with a slight hint of salt to its sweetness.

BLACK PLUM. One of my favorite Russian varieties, this produces 2- to 3-inch, elongated, plum-shaped fruit that is deep mahogany with dusky green shoulders. The fruit resembles a small paste tomato with thinner walls and has a unique, sweet, tangy flavor.

BLACK PRINCE. Originally from Siberia, this one is a fine choice for your garden. The deep garnet, round, 2-inch slicers are full of juice and incredibly rich fruity flavors. Deep, rich colors reveal themselves when you slice these tomatoes open.

Black Prince

BRADLEY. This long-time favorite pink tomato in the South produces large crops of 6- to 10-ounce round, pink tomatoes that boast of the old-fashioned tomato flavor sought by tomato lovers. This determinate is perfect for eating fresh or canning.

BRANDYWINE. Probably the first heirloom to achieve "cult status" within the growing popularity of heirloom tomatoes, this is a pink, potato-leaf, Amish variety from the 1880s. Years ago, seed saving was done by wise individuals. One such pioneer was a Vermont man named Ben Quinsenbury. He died at age ninety-five, passing on his legacy. The Brandywine was Ben's favorite tomato. In my years of holding tomato tastings for chefs and tomato lovers, the Brandywine has always placed as one of the top three favorites. Legendary for its exceptionally rich, succulent tomato flavor, its fruits are reddish-pink with light, creamy flesh. They average 12 ounces but can grow to 2 pounds.

CHEROKEE PURPLE. Of Cherokee Indian origin, this is a pre-1890 Tennessee heirloom. Sweet and rich in flavor with dusky rose-purple fruit up to 12 ounces, with slightly ridged shoulders. Its color is so dark it is often referred as a "black" tomato. Seeds for this tomato were sent to heirloom expert Craig Le Houllier in the 1980s by J. D. Green of Servierville, Tennessee, whose ancestors received the strain from local Cherokee Indians.

EVA PURPLE BALL. This nineteenth-century heirloom from the Black Forest region of Germany produces delicious, round, 2- to 3-inch, pink-purple fruit.

PAUL ROBESON. The seed for this Russian heirloom was made available by Marina Danilenko, a Moscow seeds woman. This favorite tomato was named after the operatic artist who won acclaim as an advocate of equal rights for blacks. His artistry was admired worldwide, especially in the Soviet Union. This is a "black" tomato with round fruit, borne two to a cluster and slightly flattened. Growing to 4

Paul Robeson

inches, its rich colors make it stand apart. It is dusky, dark red, with dark green shoulders with deep, red flesh in its center. This personal favorite of mine has flavorful fruits with luscious, sweet, earthy flavors and a good acid-sweet balance.

PINK ODORIKO. Considered by many to be the best Japanese hybrid, this is both a showpiece and a tasty addition to any meal. Its fruits are medium-sized and round with a distinctive deep rose-red color. They are full and mildly sweet flavored with well-balanced acid. These plants do well in most growing areas.

Purple Calabash

PURPLE CALABASH. The most purple of all the purple-black tomatoes, this 3-inch, flattened fruit is deep burgundy-purple and extremely fluted with thin skin. Its fruity flavors have a hint of red wine. Its unique appearance is a showpiece and conversation starter.

RADIATOR CHARLIE'S MORTGAGE LIFTER.
Developed by M. C. Byles in the 1930s, this
tomato remains very much in demand in the mid-
Atlantic states. Mr. Byles, affectionately known as
"Radiator Charlie," earned his nickname from the
radiator repair business he opened at the foot of a
steep hill on which trucks would often
overheat. Radiator Charlie, who
had no formal education or plant
breeding experience, created
this legendary tomato by
crossbreeding four of the largest
tomatoes he was able to find. He
developed a stable variety after
six years of pollination and selection. He then sold
his tomato plants for one dollar each (in the 1940s)
and paid off the $6,000 mortgage on his house in
six years. It is said that each spring, gardeners
drove as far as 200 miles to buy Charlie's seedling
tomatoes. The large, slightly flattened, pink-red
fruits range from ½ pound to more than 3 pounds,
and are meaty, flavorful, and have few seeds.

Radiator Charlie's Mortgage Lifter

TAPPY'S FINEST. This heirloom beefsteak from
West Virginia dates to some time before 1948. The
plant bears 1-pound dark-pink, meaty fruit with
ribbed shoulders and few seeds. Performing best
where summers are warm to cool, it is loaded with
sweet, rich flavors reminiscent of old-time tomatoes. And it makes great tomato juice.

Winsall

WINSALL. This
heirloom was named
in 1925 in a contest. A
favorite and consistent
choice year after year,
the fruit is slightly flattened, beautiful, and
rose-pink at 1 to 2
pounds. The outstand-

ing true tomatoey flavor is intense, balanced, and sweet. It is best enjoyed on its own.

Bicolored Tomatoes

BIG WHITE PINK STRIPE. This pale-peach colored, 4-inch globe slicer has a pinkish blush on the blossom end and peach-colored flesh inside. The meaty fruit has a flavor similar to a melon, but with a slight sweet-tart tang.

HILLBILLY. An Ohio heirloom beefsteak originally from West Virginia, the 1- to 2-pound orange-yellow fruit has red mottled skin and red streaks within. It is very sweet tasting, with low acid. It's attractive served in big slices with other colored tomatoes.

MARIZOL GOLD. This is another heirloom beef-steak from the Black Forest region of Germany. The round, 1- to 2-pound, deep-gold fruits with a red blush feature red streaks on blossom end and throughout inside. They have slightly ribbed shoulders, are slightly flattened, and are very seedy. The rich sweet flavor is outstanding.

Marvel Striped

MARVEL STRIPED. Originally from Oaxaca, Mexico, this beefsteak is the largest of the bi-colored tomatoes, growing over 4 inches and 2 pounds. It has a sweet, mild, fruity flavor and produces best when water and temperatures are consistent.

Pineapple

PINEAPPLE. This heirloom garden favorite boasts bicolored yellow fruit with a red blush and a yellow interior with a red starburst in center. The fruit grow to 2 pounds and are slightly flattened. They have wonderfully mild, fruity-sweet flavors.

TIGERELLA (OR MR. STRIPEY). This highly productive English vine produces beautiful, silver-dollar sized, round fruits. The red-orange skin has golden-green to yellow jagged stripes. The juicy flesh is red-orange with a brisk, tangy (tart) flavor.

Yellow and Orange Tomatoes

AMANA ORANGE. Named for Amana, Iowa, this beefsteak bears light-orange fruit that can grow to 2 pounds or more and has a mildly sweet flavor.

DAD'S SUNSET. These uniformly round, 12- to 16-ounce, golden-orange fruit are the color of the setting sun. The great sweet flavor and visual appeal make it a good choice for the home garden.

DIXIE GOLDEN GIANT. This beefsteak heirloom, which bears 1- to 2-pound, clear lemon-yellow fruits that occasionally have a pink blush on the blossom end, has a pronounced sweet, fruity taste and a meaty texture.

DR. WYCHE'S YELLOW. A slightly flattened beefsteak heirloom, this plant bears 1- to 2-pound golden-yellow fruit. The meaty interior has few seeds and is a great-tasting favorite.

EARL OF EDGECOMBE. When the sixth earl of Edgecombe died in the 1960s, the heir to the title of seventh earl was a relative in New Zealand who was a sheep farmer at the time. When he traveled to England to claim the title, he brought this tomato with him. The seed for this New Zealand heirloom was made available through Dr. Carolyn Male, who found it the best of her 1996 seed trials. The smooth 3-inch, round, uniformly ripening fruits are beautiful orange globes, typically borne in clusters of two or more. Their flesh is firm, meaty, and exceptionally flavorful.

FLAMMÉ. This extremely prolific French heirloom bears beautiful, 1½-inch, round golf–ball sized tomatoes. Persimmon-orange color inside and out makes it particularly decorative. This consistent favorite of tasters makes a great sauce.

HUGH'S. Dating to 1941, this heirloom beefsteak from Madison County, Indiana, bears 1- to 2-pound, pale-yellow fruits. They have a loyal following due to their meatiness and robust tomatoey flavor and are similar to the better-tasting red varieties.

Lemon Boy

LEMON BOY. The first lemon yellow (not golden) tomato variety is a 7-ounce, round, hybrid slicer. Much tastier than most yellow tomatoes, it's sweet but has real "backbone." This long-time friend in any garden is dependably productive.

LILLIAN'S YELLOW HEIRLOOM. This is a potato-leaf, beefsteak heirloom from Manchester, Tennessee, with 10- to 16-ounce, clear yellow, globe-shaped fruits. The fruits are mildly sweet, juicy, and rich in fruity flavors.

MANDARIN CROSS. Most yellow tomatoes are too flat tasting, but this hybrid is different. Large, solid, and gold, the gold-orange flesh has a juicy, creamy texture with a delicate fruit-sweet flavor. Try them sliced with dark-purple opal basil and olive oil for a sumptuously simple dish.

MANYEL. This name means "many moons," which is what the 3-inch, round, clear-yellow fruits look like hanging from the plant. The fruit is mildly sweet and juicy.

Persimmon

PERSIMMON. Introduced around 1983, this heirloom is another personal favorite because it has one of the best flavors of all the orange tomatoes. The rose-orange (persimmon-colored) fruits range from 12 ounces to 2 pounds. They are meaty, very sweet, and have few seeds.

PLUM LEMON. The seed for this was collected in 1991 from an old seedsman in Moscow. The fruit is pointed on the ends just like a lemon and is a bright, clear yellow. Mildly sweet, the fruit reaches about 3 inches.

SOPHIE'S CHOICE. An heirloom originally from Edmonton, Canada, this is a favorite choice for an extra-early tomato. Unlike other extra-early varieties, Sophie's Choice is very flavorful. The fruit weighs up to 12 ounces and features an orange-red exterior and a deep-red interior. The quality of this determinate is best in cool climates.

VALENCIA. This heirloom from Maine has beautiful round, 10-ounce orange fruits that contain a rich tomatoey flavor. It's a good choice for cooler growing areas.

YELLOW PEACH. This unique heirloom favorite is light yellow with a pink blush, and the Ping Pong–ball sized fruit is elegant in appearance — fuzzy like a peach and especially fragile to handle. Its light, clean, fruitlike flavor is delicate and yet charmingly distinctive.

YELLOW PERFECTION. A potato-leaf heirloom originally from an old British seed company, this plant produces 1½-inch, round, brilliant yellow, delicious fruits.

Yellow Perfection

YELLOW RUFFLED. Included in gardens because of its exciting appearance, this "stuffer" has 2- to 3-inch fruit deeply pleated like an accordion with a hollow seed cavity perfect for stuffing. It has a pleasing, mild flavor.

Other Colored Tomatoes

AUNT RUBY'S GERMAN GREEN. This heirloom beefsteak is a gift from Ruby Arnold of Greeneville, Tennessee, who passed away in 1997. The slightly flattened, 1-pound fruit ripens to a pale greenish-yellow with a slight pink blush that extends to the inside. It is superb, fruity sweet, and has a slightly spicy taste.

GREEN ZEBRA. Developed in 1985 by heirloom tomato breeder Tom Wagner, this heirloom is an unusual and exquisite tomato chosen by Alice Waters for her restaurant, Chez Panisse, in Berkeley, California. The 2-inch round fruit ripens

Green Zebra

to a yellow-gold with dark green zebralike stripes. The flesh is lime-emerald in color and has an invigorating lemon-lime flavor. This is a great tomato for brightening up salads and other tomato dishes.

WHITE QUEEN. This heirloom beefsteak produces 3-inch, pale, creamy yellow (almost white) fruit. Round and slightly flat with gently ribbed shoulders, it is juicy with a sweet, well-balanced flavor.

Paste Tomatoes

White Queen

CAROL CHYLEO'S BIG PASTE. This is a large, heart-shaped, red, meaty tomato with few seeds.

MARTINO'S ROMA. An heirloom that produces an abundant crop, its richly flavored, 3-inch, red pear tomatoes are perfect for cooking but sweet enough to enjoy fresh. This determinate is meaty with few seeds and is great for canning, adding to sauces, or making paste.

MILANO. This short, bushy, Italian hybrid bears heavy yields of deep red, long, pear-shaped meaty fruits that cook down in almost half the time of many other varieties. It's a determinate.

POWER'S HEIRLOOM. An heirloom that bears lots of clear yellow, 3- to 3½-inch long, slightly oval fruits, these beautiful tomatoes feature a light blush of pink buried in its pale yellow center. Although this is technically a paste tomato, its fruity flavor and juiciness beg for it to be eaten fresh.

ROPRECO PASTE. This determinate is a very productive, Italian (Roma-type) tomato with 2- to 3-inch, intensely red fruit. As it is one of the earliest maturing paste tomatoes, it is ideal for cooler, short-season areas and small gardens.

SAN REMO. A vigorous hybrid climbing vine bred from traditional Italian stock, this plant yields thick clusters of large sausage-shaped tomatoes that are irregularly shaped with distinctive pointy tips. The fruits hold their shape well, have few seeds, and have lots of sugar. Because their crimson pulp lacks the usual watery juice of many varieties, they are perfect for salsas, drying, or making sauce.

Tomatillos

Tomatillos grow prolifically and, if unpruned, should be spaced 4 feet apart. Just a few plants should produce enough of a harvest of ripe fruit for the most avid salsa maker. Harvest fruit when the paperlike husk loosens and turns to pale yellow. Use them fresh or cook them to invigorate any rice, Mexican, or Southwestern dish. Tomatillos freeze well, enabling you to cook with them all year long.

PURPLE TOMATILLO. The skin and flesh turn a royal purple while the husks remain a buff green. Keep harvested fruit in the light to intensify the purple color.

TOMA VERDE. This strain bears an abundance of 1½-inch, papery-husked fruits on plants that reach 4 feet across. They are appreciated for their sweet-tart flavor and are used in Southwestern dishes and salsas.

A Tasting of Tomatoes

Through most of my adult life, food tastings have been a source of great enjoyment for me. It didn't really matter so much what was being tasted. The enjoyment was based more on the process of discovery inherent in comparing characteristics of samples of the same kind of food or drink. I always came away from the experience having learned something more about the food or drink or myself. Some of my favorite tastings come to mind. I did a "Coke-Pepsi Tasting" with a large group of friends, all of whom were devoutly loyal to their respective brands. (This was during the time when "New Coke" bumped "Classic Coke" off the shelves.) I recall that some people in the group had a difficult time recovering from having their preconceptions shattered by a blind tasting. It's difficult not to come to a tasting with a bias that can easily skew your sense of taste. There

was also the "Peanut Butter Tasting" with my sons in the backyard. Then there was a "Russian/Iranian Caviar and Vintage Champagne Tasting" (wonderful), a "Tequila Tasting" (don't ask), and a "Tasting of the World's Greatest Ports" in San Francisco, where owners of the great port houses in England depleted many of their finest reserves.

So, it's not too difficult to see why, when I started harvesting my new crop of heirloom tomatoes a few years back, I thought it would be a good idea to invite a few friends over to the house for a "Tomato Tasting." We could

all discover the delights of tomatoes together and share our opinions along with good food and friendship. Quite a few of the people who joined my first tomato tasting were professional chefs. They had little time to relax with their families and, for the most part, only had Sundays off from work. Consequently, I decided to structure what became the annual TomatoFest around an outdoor barbecue on a Sunday afternoon. Everyone brought a dish that used heirloom tomatoes. The barbecued foods

would balance the menu of tomato dishes and naturally create a friendly, kicked-back atmosphere. To top it off, we had live music played by guests who brought their own musical instruments. The afternoon, the gardens, and the people were filled with music and, most importantly, a sense of

sharing the celebration of a splendid tomato harvest.

If you decide to do a tomato tasting, whether for six or sixty, I encourage you to make it a family event that includes people of all ages. I think the moments I've most enjoyed at tomato tastings were observing young children, fascinated by their own discovery of new flavors, in serious discourse with one another about their favorites: "I like this one best!" and "You haven't tried this one!" But it's usually most comfortable for all your guests to refrain from getting too serious and formal about the process of tasting and taking notes. Above all, this experience is intended to be fun!

Dwarf White

The tomatoes tasted can either be different varieties from your own garden or you can include tomatoes contributed from your guests' gardens. If your guests are bringing one or more varieties, ask ahead of time the name and description of the variety so you can include this information on your list of tomatoes.

Over years of holding tomato tastings for professional cooks and friends who share my passion for great-tasting tomatoes, I've kept track of the overall favorites. Here (in alphabetical order), from the last three years of tastings, are the top twelve varieties that were consistently chosen. (Brandywine has placed first every year.)

Big Beef
Black Prince
Brandywine
Carmello
Dona
Enchantment
Green Zebra
Mandarin Cross
Marmande
Paul Robeson
Stupice
Sun Gold

Reaping the Harvest

Stretching the Harvest

Since I grow indeterminate varieties, which continue to push out fruit until the first few cold snaps of late fall, I always seem to have green tomatoes hanging from the vines when it's time to pull them from the ground.

You can pick all the fruit that is light green or slightly ripened to continue ripening indoors. They won't be as flavorful as the vine-ripe tomatoes you got used to over the summer, but they are likely to be just as good, if not better, than the ones in the market that are shipped in from somewhere else.

Aside from the natural choice of using these green tomatoes for Green Tomato Salsa, Green Tomato Pie, Fried Green Tomatoes (see recipe section), or any other delicious condiment, you can turn these green tomatoes into ripe tomatoes. If you are lucky enough to have an adequate space (i.e., a back porch, pantry, root cellar, shed, or even garage) that is protected from cold weather, you can pull up the last of your plants by the roots, with green tomatoes still attached, and hang them upside down. Although the rate of ripening will slow dramatically, you can enjoy picking tomatoes for another two or three weeks. Any fruit that doesn't turn ripe can be used for green tomato recipes.

If you have no such space available or this sounds like too much to deal with, you might try leaving your plants in the ground and covering

them with anything that is lightweight enough to keep from damaging the plant. If you are covering the plants during the day, as well as night, the material should be transparent, like a clear plastic.

Drying

Purchasing sundried tomatoes can be expensive. But if you have tomatoes from your own garden, you might as well dry them yourself and be assured of having more flavorful tomatoes to start with. Drying concentrates the delicious sweet-tart flavor.

If you intend to dry tomatoes for more than one season, you might want to consider buying a dehydrator. If the climate you live in is hot and dry, go ahead and try producing sundried tomatoes the old-fashioned way, like they still do in Italy.

Select some different varieties (including different colors) for drying. Any tomato will do, but you may wish to stay away from the exceptionally juicy ones because they will take longer to dry out. (Some of my favorites for drying are Principe Borghese, San Marzano, San Remo, Flammé, Aunt Ruby's German Green, and Persimmon.) The thinner you slice the tomatoes, the quicker they will dry. I've found that a ¼-inch slice is ideal.

You can improvise makeshift racks for sun drying your tomatoes. Just be sure that there is adequate air circulating above and below the tomatoes. A plastic window screen or muslin stretched over a frame will work well. I like to cover the tomatoes with cheesecloth to keep the bugs off. Turn the tomatoes every day. It should take only three or four days before they start to look like soft leather. If you live on the coast, where the nights are cool and moist, you may have to bring them indoors or put a plastic tent over them to protect them from the moisture. If you are set upon by cooler days, you may need to finish the drying process in the oven. If so, put the tomatoes

in the oven warmed to 150 to 200 degrees on a
ventilated rack. Then, you may either turn off the
heat and let them set a day or so, until they are soft
and leathery, or keep the heat on for two or more
hours to finish. If it is warm and dry enough, you
can dry your tomatoes without the fear of invading
mold. If there is any indication of mold on your
tomatoes when you finish drying, toss them out.

Store your sundried tomatoes in air-tight
containers or freeze them. I prefer to store mine
in plastic bags in the freezer (where I can retrieve
any amount when needed) or pack them in sterile
jars and cover them with a good extra virgin olive
oil, with fresh rosemary added. This way you will
have a flavorful oil to use, as well as the sundried,
oil-soaked tomatoes.

Canning

Homemade canned goods still remind me of another
era—when family life was centered around garden
and kitchen. Canning is my preferred method of
preserving the summer's taste of heirloom tomatoes.
I do it the old-fashioned way, which is still a viable
method today, using glass canning jars in a boiling
water bath.

When harvesting your tomatoes, select only
those that are fully ripe. Peel the tomatoes (see
pages 78–79) and save any resulting juices. Leave
them whole or cut them into chunks and put them
into sterilized jars, allowing about ⅝-inch headroom
space from the top of the rim. Proceed with canning instructions that can be found in almost any
all-purpose cookbook or that come with the canning
jars you purchase.

Canning your harvest is dependably easy and
safe. But follow the directions for procedures.
Timing is very important in order to avoid creating
any toxins that could cause botulism. Canned
tomatoes and tomato sauce store well for long

periods of time. But when pulling any canned food from storage, check to see that the seal is still tight. If not, throw any questionable jars away.

Freezing

Often, when I'm in the middle of harvesting tomatoes, I find I have picked more ripe tomatoes than I can deliver to others or eat myself. And if I don't have the time to prepare a sauce or can them, the easiest way to save the tomatoes for a later date is to freeze them whole, uncooked.

When freezing fresh tomatoes, use only perfect, ripe fruit. Wash, dry, and pack them into freezer bags. When you're ready for these tomatoes, take them from the freezer bags, let them soak in cool water for a minute or two (the skins will come off easily), cut up the tomatoes and add them to a sauce or whatever recipe that calls for them.

I make lots of tomato sauce during the harvest season. Freezing what was harvested ripe that summer's day captures the delicious summer flavor to enjoy in the dead of winter. Although I prefer canning my tomato sauce for friends, I generally freeze tomato sauce for my own kitchen use throughout the nonharvest seasons. Use clear, 16-ounce, commercial plastic containers. One-quart freezer bags also work well but are more difficult to stack in the freezer. The frozen sauce can be conveniently slipped into a microwave oven for a few minutes and then enjoyed as is or added to a multitude of dishes.

You can also freeze the "water" that occurs when cooking a large quantity of tomato sauce.

This (clear to pink) water occurs when slowly cooking down different kinds of juicy (versus paste) tomatoes. It will condense and float on the top of the sauce. I used to take this water off and throw it away. But now I freeze it separately and use it as a tasty stock whenever I want a seasoned, tomatoey flavor.

To Seed or Not to Seed?

Many experienced chefs fervently believe in peeling and seeding tomatoes before using them in any cooked dish. This belief is founded in good theory, because leaving seeds in a tomato sauce may impart a bitter aftertaste. If the peels are left on when tomatoes are cooked, they too may impart an undesirable flavor and will toughen up into unsightly, annoying little curls that get caught in your teeth. The recipes in this book call for the peeling and seeding of tomatoes in cooked dishes in order to retain the clearest and most pure essence of tomato. Peeling and seeding may not be necessary when you intend to strain them out before cooking or use the tomatoes in a fresh, uncooked recipe like a salad or salsas. Don't fret over this issue. Just exercise your best judgment, taste the seeds, and decide how sweet the tomatoes you're using really are.

Peeling and seeding is simple. All you need is a pot of boiling water and a bowl of ice water. With a sharp knife, score the skins of the tomatoes in a X on the blossom ends (as opposed to the stem ends). Place them in boiling water for 15 to 20 seconds. This may be done in batches if you have a quantity of tomatoes. Plunge the tomatoes into a bowl of iced water (large enough to hold them and plenty of ice cubes). This will stop the cooking process. Slip the peel off and remove any hard cores. Cut in half and gently squeeze out the seeds. You may use a spoon to remove those little seeds that hide away.

*J. Pope "Olive" tomatoes,
harvested for pickling*

If you have a gas stove, there's another good method of peeling tomatoes when you want to impart a "smoked" flavor to a dish. Spear a tomato onto a long-handled fork and hold it over a high flame. Turn it around until the skin is charred all over, for about 30 seconds. Let the tomato cool, then peel the skin off. This method is often used in Southwestern cooking.

Generally speaking, 1 pound of ripe, unpeeled tomatoes will yield about 2 cups of peeled, seeded, and chopped tomatoes. It's always wise to begin with a little more than you think you'll need, since peeling and seeding will reduce the amount of tomatoes you end up with.

Recipes

Fresh Mozzarella with Tomato Tapenade and Basil-Infused Oil

Serves 4 as a first course or 8 as an appetizer

Be sure the mozzarella is the kind that's packed in water or fresh from your Italian deli. The rubbery kind, shrink-wrapped in plastic won't do. The fragrant, emerald green Basil-Infused Oil is a wonderful contrast to the piquant tapenade and the mild mozzarella. Use this versatile oil wherever you want — in salads or over grilled fish or vegetables.

1 pound red or gold Roma tomatoes, quartered
    lengthwise and hard cores removed
4 tablespoons extra virgin olive oil
1 tablespoon herbes de Provence
Salt and freshly ground black pepper, to taste
1 large clove garlic, chopped
1 pound fresh mozzarella
Fresh basil leaves for garnish
4 tablespoons Basil-Infused Oil
    (recipe follows)

photo on page 80: *Lemon Boy*

Preheat the oven to 200°. Place the tomatoes on parchment paper in a sheet pan in a single layer. Drizzle 2 tablespoons of the olive oil and sprinkle the herbes de Provence, salt, and pepper over them. Bake the tomatoes for 3 to 4½ hours, or until their edges shrivel up and centers are still slightly moist. Transfer them to a plate to cool.

In a food processor fitted with a metal blade, blend the dried tomatoes, garlic, and the remaining 2 tablespoons of olive oil until finely chopped. Season again with salt and pepper.

Slice the mozzarella into rounds, spread a little of the tomato tapenade on each round, and drizzle with the Basil-Infused Oil. Garnish with the basil leaves.

Basil-Infused Oil

3 tablespoons coarse salt

3 cups fresh basil leaves (packed)

1 cup olive oil

In a large saucepan, bring 4 quarts of water and the salt to a boil. Place the basil leaves in a strainer or pasta basket and immerse in the boiling water for 15 seconds. Remove and immediately plunge the strainer into a large bowl of ice water to stop the cooking and set the color. Squeeze all the excess water from the basil.

Place the olive oil and basil in a blender and blend for 3 minutes. Strain the oil through dampened cheesecloth. Store in an airtight jar, refrigerated, for up to 3 weeks.

from Brandon Miller, chef, Stokes Adobe Restaurant, Monterey, California

Fried Green Tomatoes

Serves 4 to 6

These delectable fried green tomatoes have been a featured item of the TomatoFest since its humble beginnings. The tart bite of a green tomato is mellowed by the slow pan frying, and the crisp crust gives way to the meltingly tender heart of summer.

2 pounds green tomatoes (unripe tomatoes)
½ cup flour
1 cup cornmeal
½ teaspoon salt
¾ teaspoon sugar
½ teaspoon garlic powder
½ teaspoon lemon pepper
1½ teaspoon cayenne
¼ teaspoon black pepper
2 large eggs
2 tablespoons water
¼ cup extra virgin olive oil
2 tablespoons butter

Slice the tomatoes in rounds about ⅜-inch to ½-inch thick. In a low bowl, mix together the flour, cornmeal, salt, sugar, garlic powder, lemon pepper, cayenne, and black pepper. In another bowl, whisk together the eggs and water.

Heat the olive oil and butter in a large heavy frying pan over a medium-high heat. Dredge each slice in the flour mixture first, then in the egg wash, and then in the flour mixture again. Fry the tomato slices until golden brown, watching carefully to make sure you don't scorch them. As they are done, place them on paper towels or brown paper bags, to drain excess oil.

from Gary Ibsen

Roma Goat Cheese Tarts

Makes 2 9-inch tarts

The joining of tomato with basil is the proverbial match made in heaven. Add the exciting flavor of goat cheese, put it all on a tender pine nut crust, and you have an entrée worthy of rave reviews.

¾ cup pine nuts

2 cups whole-wheat flour

1 cup all-purpose flour

2 teaspoons minced fresh thyme leaves

1 teaspoon salt

⅔ cup butter, cut in small pieces

⅔ cup solid white vegetable shortening

½ cup water, ice cold

1¼ pounds Roma tomatoes, tough cores removed and cut in ⅛-inch slices

3 large eggs

½ cup loosely packed fresh basil leaves, finely minced

1 clove garlic, finely minced

8 ounces goat cheese

1 cup heavy whipping cream

Toast the pine nuts in a 350° oven in a shallow pan for 5 to 7 minutes, or until golden brown. Let cool and coarsely chop.

In a medium bowl, combine the whole-wheat flour, all-purpose flour, thyme, and salt. With a pastry blender or your fingers, rub the butter and shortening into the flour until the mixture is the

size of peas. Mix in the pine nuts. With a fork, gently stir in about ½ cup ice-cold water, 1 table-spoon at a time, just until the dough adheres together. Gather the dough into a ball, divide in half, and shape each portion into flat disks. Wrap tightly in plastic wrap and chill at least 45 minutes, or up to 2 days.

Preheat the oven to 375°. On a board dusted with all-purpose flour, roll the dough into 11-inch rounds. Fit each round into a 9-inch tart pan with a removable bottom. Trim the excess dough from the edges. Fit a piece of aluminum foil into each crust, place dried beans or pie weights on the foil, and bake for 20 minutes. Remove the foil and beans.

Overlap the tomato slices in concentric circles onto the hot crusts. Bake for 10 to 15 minutes, until the tomatoes look dry at the edges. (Check to make sure the tomatoes don't overcook—you just want them to lose some of their moisture.)

Meanwhile, in a medium bowl, whisk the eggs, basil, and garlic together until thoroughly blended. Blend in the goat cheese and cream. Gently pour this custard mixture over the tomatoes in the crusts. Bake the tarts for another 20 to 25 minutes, or until the custard seems set when the tarts are gently shaken. Serve hot or cold.

from Lisa Magadini, executive chef, Club XIX, Pebble Beach Resort, Carmel, California

Tomato Seafood Shooters

Makes 25 to 30 shooters

These delectable tomato-and-seafood-packed shot glasses are great fun to slurp. Use any seafood you like — shrimp, octopus (surprisingly great here), squid, crab, lobster, or clams. Or better yet, use a combination of seafood for a sensational shooter!

1 medium yellow onion, sliced

2 stalks celery, chopped

1 bay leaf, ½ teaspoon whole peppercorns and
    3 sprigs parsley, tied into a cheesecloth bag

1 lemon, sliced

2 cups water

1 cup white wine

2 teaspoons salt

2 pounds (cooked weight) seafood, such as
    shrimp, octopus, squid, crab, lobster, or clams

1½ pounds red tomatoes, peeled, seeded,
    and puréed (about 3 cups)

½ cup diced avocado

½ cup diced tomato

½ cup diced red onion

½ cup diced cucumber

½ cup freshly squeezed lime juice

2 serrano chile peppers, thinly sliced

¼ cup extra virgin olive oil

½ bunch cilantro, chopped

2 cups premium tequila (optional)

Combine the onion, celery, bay leaf, peppercorns, parsley, lemon, water, wine, and salt in a saucepan. Bring to a boil. Add the seafood of choice and cook accordingly. (For shrimp, cook until the shrimp turns pink, 2 to 3 minutes, peel and devein. For octopus, lower the heat and simmer for 35 to 40 minutes, or until tender. For cleaned squid, cook for just 1 minute or it will toughen. For crab or lobster, cook until the shell turns red, about 12 to 15 minutes, pick the meat out and discard shells. For clams, cook until the shells open, about 5 minutes, save the meat and discard the shells.) Remove the seafood from the broth and let cool. Dice the seafood and set aside.

Add the 3 cups puréed tomatoes (alternately, you may use canned tomato juice) to the broth and simmer 30 minutes or until reduced by half. Strain the broth, pressing down on the solids to extract all the liquid. Discard the solids. (You should end up with about 2 cups of tomato broth.) Cool completely.

Pour the tomato broth into a glass pitcher. Stir in the diced seafood, avocado, tomato, red onion, cucumber, lime juice, serrano chiles, olive oil, and cilantro. Place in the refrigerator, covered with plastic wrap, until well chilled. Serve in shot glasses. You may stir the optional tequila into the pitcher, or float a little tequila on top of each shot glass.

from Drew Previti, chef, Bay Club Restaurant, The Inn at Spanish Bay, Pebble Beach, California

Tomato Kissel and Vanilla-Basil Cream

Serves 6 to 8

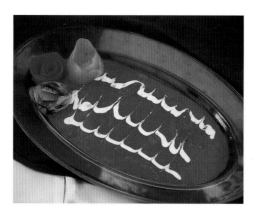

This is an incredibly different soup. It's an ideal first-course soup or a light dessert soup to finish a heavy dinner. But either way you enjoy it, like summer itself, it's pure ambrosia that's sure to be talked about long after it's gone.

4 cups fresh tomato juice, or substitute
    canned tomato juice
½ cup sugar, or to taste
6 tablespoons potato flour
1 pound yellow tomatoes, peeled, seeded,
    and chopped
1 pound red tomatoes, peeled, seeded,
    and chopped
2 teaspoons prepared horseradish
Salt and freshly ground black pepper, to taste
Vanilla-Basil Cream (recipe follows)

Combine the tomato juice and sugar in a medium saucepan over a medium-low heat. (If the tomato juice is sweet tasting, you won't need more sugar. You don't want the kissel overly sweet.) Mix in the potato flour. Stirring constantly, simmer for about 5 minutes. Remove from the heat. Stir in the chopped tomatoes and horseradish. Season with salt and pepper. Pour into a serving bowl and chill in the refrigerator to allow the flavors to meld. Pour the Vanilla-Basil Cream into a squirt bottle and "squirt" a decorative squiggle of cream on top of each bowl of Tomato Kissel.

Vanilla-Basil Cream

1 cup low-fat cottage cheese

1 cup low-fat yogurt

⅓ cup powdered sugar

½ teaspoon vanilla extract

¼ cup of basil leaves, finely chopped

Blend all of the ingredients in blender or food processor until smooth. Store in an airtight container in the refrigerator until ready to serve.

From Jim Gallivan, Fess Parker's Wine Country Inn, Los Olivos, California

Old-Fashioned Tomato Cream Soup

Serves 4 to 6

The key to this nostalgic soup is thoughtful preparation. Easily done, the care taken in making this soup will come back in thankful reward. Try partnering this soup with a crispy grilled cheese sandwich made with a good sharp Cheddar.

2½ pounds ripe red tomatoes, peeled, seeded, and chopped

1 medium onion, studded with 10 whole cloves

1¼ cups beef stock

2 tablespoons chopped fresh basil

2 teaspoons salt

½ teaspoon freshly ground black pepper

¼ teaspoon ground nutmeg

¼ teaspoon ground coriander

¼ teaspoon baking soda

2 teaspoons sugar

2 tablespoons flour

2 tablespoons butter, softened

1½ cups heavy whipping cream, heated almost to boiling

Fresh basil leaves, julienned, for garnish

In a large deep saucepan, over a medium heat, cook the tomatoes, onion, beef stock, basil, salt and pepper, nutmeg, and coriander for 30 minutes. Let cool a little, then remove and discard the cloves from the onions. Purée the soup in a blender until smooth. (This may be done in batches.) Return the soup to the saucepan and stir in the baking soda and sugar. Blend the flour and butter together to form a smooth paste. Stir this into the soup.

Watching carefully, cook the soup, over a medium-low heat, until thickened, 10 to 15 minutes. Remove the saucepan from the heat and slowly stir in the warmed cream. Return the soup to the heat and continue to warm it, just until it is piping hot and about to come to a boil. (Don't let it boil or it will curdle and truly disappoint you!) Serve this soup garnished with fresh basil leaves.

from Dale Ann Feuerman, Howard Portnoy Gallery, Carmel, California

Dona

Arabian Gazpacho

Serves 4 to 6

The use of cumin, coriander, cilantro, and mint in this gazpacho highlights the Arabian influence in Spanish cuisine. It is refreshing, delicious, and even thirst-quenching.

3 tablespoons extra virgin olive oil

4 to 5 cloves garlic, finely chopped

1 tablespoon sweet paprika

2 teaspoons ground cumin

1 teaspoon ground coriander

¼ teaspoon cayenne, or to taste

2½ pounds ripe red tomatoes

2 tablespoons sherry wine vinegar

2 tablespoons freshly squeezed lemon juice

3 tablespoons chopped fresh cilantro

1 tablespoon chopped fresh mint

2 teaspoons salt

Freshly ground black pepper, to taste

Warm the olive oil in a small sauté pan over a low heat. Stir in the garlic, paprika, cumin, coriander, and cayenne and sauté for 2 to 3 minutes. Remove from the heat and let the mixture cool. Core and cut the tomatoes into chunks. Pass them through a food mill fitted with a coarse disk. Or, push the tomatoes through a medium strainer with a wooden mallet or spoon. Discard the peels and seeds. Place the tomatoes in a bowl and stir in the spice mixture and the vinegar, lemon juice, cilantro, mint, salt, and pepper. Thin, if necessary, with a little cold water. Cover and chill for at least an hour before serving to let the flavors meld.

from Joan Nielsen

Ensalada de Tomates Coloridos con Camarones

(Tricolored Tomato Salad with Shrimp)

Serves 6 to 8

Shrimp seems to be the one thing guests can never get enough of. This delectable shrimp salad is chock full of multicolored tomatoes and shrimp, tossed with red onion, fresh herbs, and a minced jalapeño pepper, and finished with a zesty dressing of lime, garlic, cumin, and coriander.

1 cup plus 2 tablespoons olive oil

2 pounds large shrimp, peeled and deveined

1 basket (about 7 ounces) red cherry tomatoes, rinsed and halved

1 basket (about 7 ounces) yellow cherry tomatoes, rinsed and halved

6 small tomatillos, husks removed, rinsed, and quartered

1 medium red onion, diced

1 jalapeño pepper, finely chopped

¼ cup chopped fresh cilantro

¼ cup chopped fresh parsley

½ cup freshly squeezed lime juice

1 teaspoon minced garlic

1 teaspoon cumin seeds, lightly toasted

1 teaspoon coriander seeds, lightly toasted

½ teaspoon cayenne pepper

½ tablespoon Dijon mustard

Salt and freshly ground black pepper, to taste

Heat 1 tablespoon of the olive oil in a large sauté pan over a medium heat. Sauté 1 pound of the shrimp for 2 to 3 minutes, or until shrimp have just turned pink. Set aside to cool. Heat 1 more tablespoon of the olive oil and sauté the remaining pound of shrimp until done. Add to the other shrimp to cool.

In a large bowl, combine all of the tomatoes, the red onion, jalapeño pepper, cilantro, parsley, and the cooked shrimp. Toss well and place on a large decorative serving platter or on individual plates.

In a small bowl, thoroughly mix together the lime juice, garlic, cumin, coriander, cayenne pepper, and mustard. Whisk in the remaining 1 cup of olive oil a little at a time until it is completely incorporated. Drizzle this dressing over the salad. Season to taste with salt and pepper.

from Ana Machado, executive chef at PortaBella and Café Americana, Carmel, California

Tomato Aspic with Spring Dressing

Serves 6 to 8

This dish just bursts with the concentrated flavor of tomato. Serve it with some deviled eggs, a leafy green salad, and toasted rough country bread for an unforgettably wonderful snack—luxurious but simple.

2 pounds ripe red tomatoes, peeled, seeded, and
  chopped (or 3¾ cups canned tomato juice)
1 small stalk of celery, with green leaves, chopped
½ small onion, chopped
1 to 2 tablespoons sugar, depending on the
  sweetness of the tomatoes
1 sprig parsley
1 bay leaf
2 envelopes gelatin, softened in ⅓ cup cold water
½ teaspoon Worcestershire sauce
Dash of Tabasco sauce
2 tablespoons freshly squeezed lemon juice,
  or more, to taste
½ teaspoon salt
Freshly ground white pepper, to taste
Spring Dressing (recipe follows)

Pass the tomatoes through a food mill fitted with a fine disk. Or, push the tomatoes through a fine strainer with a wooden spoon. You should have about 3¾ cups of tomato juice. In a small saucepan, place the tomato juice, celery, onion, sugar to taste, parsley, and bay leaf. Cook over a medium-low heat until just beginning to boil, 5 to 7 minutes. Remove from the heat and stir in the gelatin until dissolved. Stir in the Worcestershire, Tabasco, lemon juice, salt, and white pepper. Strain the liquid and discard the solids. Measure the aspic mixture. You should have about 4 cups. Add a little more tomato juice, if necessary. Chill the aspic in any decorative mold or glass bowl until firm. Serve with Spring Dressing.

Note: You can use this recipe with any color tomatoes you may have on hand—red, yellow, orange, or green. Repeat the recipe for each color of tomato. Then layer the colors in a loaf pan or decorative mold, after each is just starting to gel, for a spectacular presentation.

Spring Dressing

½ cup mayonnaise, preferably homemade

2 green onions, finely chopped, white and
   green parts included

1 small clove garlic, finely minced

2 tablespoons finely chopped fresh chives

1 tablespoon finely chopped fresh parsley

1 tablespoon freshly squeezed lemon juice

Salt and freshly ground black pepper, to taste

In a small bowl, combine all of the ingredients until well mixed. Allow it to chill at least an hour for the flavors to meld. Store in an airtight jar, refrigerated, for up 1 week.

from Joan Nielsen

Tomato Skewers with Asian Slaw and Ginger-Wasabi Aioli

Serves 4 to 8

The presentation of this salad is spectacular. The Asian Slaw is dressed with a sweet and sour vinaigrette, a perfect foil to the smooth, cool mozzarella and tomato skewers. The creamy yet pungent aioli is flavored with wasabi (a Japanese horseradish) and ginger.

8 medium- to small-sized heirloom tomatoes
    of different colors, quartered
24 mini, fresh mozzarella balls (packed in water),
    or larger fresh mozzarella cut in ½-inch pieces
24 basil leaves
Asian Slaw and Vinaigrette (recipe follows)
Ginger-Wasabi Aioli (recipe follows)

On 8 6-inch bamboo skewers, starting with a tomato quarter, alternate 4 tomato quarters with 3 mozzarella balls and 3 basil leaves. To serve, place the slaw on a large serving platter or on individual plates. Arrange the skewers on top of the slaw. Squirt, or drizzle, the Ginger-Wasabi Aioli decoratively over all.

Asian Slaw and Vinaigrette

½ head shredded green cabbage

1 bunch cilantro, coarsely chopped

1 medium red bell pepper, cut in thin
　　matchstick strips

1 medium carrot, cut in thin matchstick strips

1 tablespoon tomato paste

1 tablespoon wasabi powder

1 tablespoon ground ginger

1 tablespoon soy sauce

¼ cup sugar

¼ cup freshly squeezed lemon juice

½ cup rice wine vinegar

¾ cup vegetable oil

In a large bowl, toss together the cabbage, cilantro,
bell pepper, and carrot. Cover and refrigerate until
ready to serve. (This may be prepared in advance.)
In a small bowl, combine the tomato paste, wasabi
powder, ginger, and soy sauce. Stir in the sugar,
lemon juice, and vinegar until the sugar is dissolved.
Whisk in the oil until thoroughly combined. (This
may be prepared in advance.) When ready to serve,
toss the slaw with the vinaigrette.

Ginger-Wasabi Aioli

1 tablespoon wasabi powder

1 tablespoon ground ginger

¼ cup sour cream

¼ cup mayonnaise

In a small mixing bowl, blend the wasabi, ginger,
sour cream, and mayonnaise. If you can, place
the aioli in a squirt bottle.

**from Bill Lee, Billy Quon's Restaurant,
Monterey, California**

Tuscan Tomato Bread Salad

Serves 8 to 12

Add roasted and peeled red, yellow, and green peppers if you really want to dress this up, but come-as-you-are, this is a beautiful, big-flavored, savory salad that begs for a repeat performance.

2½ pounds mixed heirloom tomatoes, peeled and seeded, or substitute 2 (28-ounce) cans drained, Italian-style whole tomatoes, roughly chopped

1 loaf rustic country bread

1 cup extra virgin olive oil

¼ cup red wine vinegar

1 large clove garlic, chopped

Salt and freshly ground black pepper, to taste

½ cup extra large capers

2 (2-ounce) cans anchovies

½ cup packed black oil-cured olives

1 bunch baby spinach, stemmed, thoroughly washed, and dried

1 bunch basil, stemmed, rinsed, and dried, large leaves torn in pieces

Cut the tomatoes in ½-inch chunks, reserving all juice. Set aside the tomatoes in a strainer, over a medium bowl, to catch more juice. Cut the bread in 1-inch cubes, toast lightly, and set aside.

To the reserved tomato juice, thoroughly whisk in the olive oil, vinegar, garlic, salt, and pepper. Set this vinaigrette aside.

Fry the capers in a little olive oil, over a low heat, until crisp. Use care not to burn them. Place them on paper towels to drain. Pour the oil off the anchovies, place them on paper towels and pat dry. Pit and halve the black olives. Set aside.

In a large decorative bowl or deep platter, toss the chopped tomatoes, bread, vinaigrette, spinach and basil, until well blended. Garnish with the capers, anchovies, and black olives. Serve at room temperature.

from Brandon Miller, chef, Stokes Adobe Restaurant, Monterey, California

Tortellini with Oven-Dried Tomatoes and Eggplant Croutons

Serves 6

The beauty of this dish is that almost all of the components can be prepared in advance—the tortellini, the oven-dried tomatoes, and the Basil-Balsamic Vinaigrette. You have only to make the eggplant croutons at the last minute and toss the whole thing together for a wonderfully different main course.

1 pound fresh Gorgonzola-filled tortellini
2 tablespoon extra virgin olive oil
Oven-dried tomatoes (recipe follows)
Basil-Balsamic Vinaigrette (recipe follows)
Eggplant croutons (recipe follows)
Sprigs Italian flat-leaf parsley for garnish

In a medium saucepan, cook the tortellini in boiling, salted water for about 5 minutes. Drain and rinse quickly in cold water to stop the cooking process. Drain well and toss with the olive oil.

When ready to serve, toss the tortellini and tomatoes with the vinaigrette. Garnish with eggplant croutons and sprigs of Italian parsley. Serve immediately.

Oven-Dried Tomatoes

2 pounds Roma tomatoes, quartered lengthwise
    and hard cores removed
2 tablespoons salt

Preheat the oven to 200°. Place the tomatoes on parchment paper in a sheet pan in a single layer. Sprinkle with the 2 tablespoons salt. Bake the tomatoes for 3 to 4½ hours, or until most of their moisture has evaporated, the edges shrivel up, and the centers are still slightly moist. Transfer the tomatoes to a plate to cool.

Basil-Balsamic Vinaigrette

2 teaspoon chopped fresh basil
½ cup vinegar
1 tablespoon Dijon mustard
2 tablespoon powdered sugar
1 tablespoon chopped shallots
1 teaspoon chopped garlic
1 cup olive oil
½ teaspoon salt
½ teaspoon freshly ground black pepper

Place the basil, vinegar, mustard, sugar, shallots, and garlic in a blender. Blend for 20 seconds. While blending, slowly add the olive oil. Add the salt and pepper. Set aside, covered, until ready to use.

Eggplant Croutons

1 large eggplant (about 1 to 1½ pounds)
Salt and freshly ground black pepper, to taste
1½ tablespoons granulated garlic

Cut the eggplants into ¾-inch cubes, leaving the
skin on. Place in a large bowl of salted water for
½ hour. Drain well and pat dry. Sprinkle with salt,
pepper, and granulated garlic. Deep fry in
vegetable oil at 320° until golden brown. Drain
on paper towels.

**from Bert Cutino, The Sardine Factory,
Monterey, California**

Authentic Ragù Bolognese Sauce for Pasta

Serves 6 to 8

This luscious, rich, and satisfying sauce will remind you of the way food used to taste, a far cry from mass-produced, bottled *ragù*. Serve it over a rustic pasta and be generous with freshly grated Parmesan. Use it as the sauce base for any baked pasta dish, like lasagne. It freezes perfectly—so take advantage of the bounty of summer tomatoes and make extra for use in the dead of winter, just when you might need it most.

4 tablespoons butter

3 tablespoons extra virgin olive oil

1 medium onion, finely chopped

3 large cloves garlic, finely chopped

2 medium carrots, finely chopped

1 stalk celery, finely chopped

1½ pounds ground beef (7 percent fat)

1½ teaspoons dried oregano

1 teaspoon dried basil

1 teaspoon dried rosemary, crushed

¾ teaspoon fennel seeds, crushed

¼ teaspoon crushed red pepper flakes

Pinch of cloves

1 cup good red wine, such as Chianti Classico or Beaujolais

2 cups peeled, seeded, and chopped plum
tomatoes (about 1 pound), or 1 (16-ounce)
can tomato pieces in juice

2 cups fresh Classic Tomato Sauce (see page 133),
or 1 (16-ounce) can tomato sauce

¼ cup tomato paste

Salt and freshly ground black pepper, to taste

½ pound mushrooms, sliced

2 tablespoons chopped fresh Italian
flat leaf parsley

Heat 1 tablespoon of the butter and all of the olive
oil in a large deep sauté pan over a medium heat.
Add the onion and garlic and sauté for 3 to 4
minutes, or until the onion is transparent. Add the
carrots and celery and sauté 3 minutes more.
Increase the heat to medium-high, add the beef,
and sauté until the beef begins to brown, breaking
up all clumps of meat with a fork. Add the oregano,
basil, rosemary, fennel, red pepper, and cloves.
Add the wine and sauté until most of the liquid has
evaporated.

Add the tomatoes, tomato sauce, and tomato paste
and stir to combine well. Lower the heat, cover, and
simmer for 1½ hours, checking to make sure the
sauce has enough liquid to keep it moist and thick.
Add a little water, if necessary. Season with salt
and pepper.

Finish the sauce by heating the remaining 3 tablespoons of butter in a small saucepan, over a
medium heat. Add the sliced mushrooms and cook
until the liquid the mushrooms exudes has
evaporated. Fold the mushrooms and parsley into
the sauce before serving.

from Joan Nielsen

Savory Clafouti of Tomatoes and Roasted Corn

Serves 6 to 8

A clafouti is a country-French puffed pancake that's traditionally served as a dessert. Here, it is given a twist with savory ingredients — fresh tomatoes, garlicky corn, pepper-flavored vodka, lemon rind, and a dusting of Parmesan. Serve it for supper, hot from the oven, and get ready for requests for encores.

1 clove garlic, minced

2 tablespoons olive oil

3 ears of corn, shucked

4 cups peeled, seeded, and chopped tomatoes
    (about 2 pounds)

4 tablespoons plus 1⅓ cup sugar

4 tablespoons pepper-flavored vodka

1 cup butter

6 large eggs

2 tablespoons freshly grated lemon zest

2 cups all-purpose flour

Salt and freshly ground black pepper, to taste

2 ounces Parmesan, grated

Mix the garlic clove with the olive oil. Rub the garlic mixture all over the corn, wrap in foil, and bake in a 350° oven for 5 minutes. Remove the kernels from the cob and set aside. (This may be done ahead of time.)

Preheat the oven to 400°. Combine the corn, tomatoes, the 4 tablespoons sugar, and vodka in a medium bowl and set aside. In another medium bowl, beat the butter and the 1⅓ cup sugar with an electric mixer until light and fluffy. Beat in the eggs one at a time. Add the lemon zest and flour. Season with salt and pepper.

Pour a thin layer of the batter into a shallow baking dish, about 8 by 13 by 2 inches and sprinkle the tomato-corn mixture evenly on top. Cover with the remaining batter. Bake for 5 minutes, then reduce the heat to 375° and bake for 40 to 45 minutes. Sprinkle the Parmesan on top of the clafouti about 5 minutes before removing from the oven. Serve immediately.

from Jim Gallivan, Fess Parker's Wine Country Inn, Los Olivos, California

Quick Cherry Tomato Pasta Sauce

Serves 4

Cook about half of a pound (dry weight) of your favorite pasta and have it ready to go in a warmed pasta bowl before you make the sauce. This dish comes together quickly, with a fresh, picked-from-the-garden flavor and an amazing show of red, yellow, and green colors.

2 tablespoons extra virgin olive oil

2 tablespoons unsalted butter

1 large clove garlic, finely chopped

½ pound red cherry tomatoes, rinsed
   and dried

½ pound yellow cherry tomatoes, rinsed
   and dried

1 bunch green onions (about 5 or 6), coarsely
   chopped, white and green parts included

3 tablespoons coarsely chopped mixed fresh
   herbs, such as basil, parsley, and chives

Salt and freshly ground black pepper, to taste

Freshly grated Parmesan or Romano cheese

Heat the olive oil and butter in a large sauté pan over a medium heat. Add the garlic and sauté 2 to 3 minutes. Add the red and yellow cherry tomatoes and sauté 2 to 3 minutes. Add the green onions, herbs, and salt and pepper. Constantly shaking the pan to mix everything together, sauté the mixture until about half of the tomatoes are beginning to burst, 5 to 7 minutes more. Remove from the heat immediately and toss the tomato sauce with the pasta. Top with freshly grated cheese.

from Joan Nielsen

Dark Cherry

Stuffed Tomatoes with Dungeness Crab and Sweet Corn

Serves 6

Succulent Dungeness crab pairs perfectly with sweet seasonal corn, serving as an excellent stuffing for a vine-ripened red tomato. Add a salad of wild baby greens, chopped hazelnuts, and blue cheese dressed with a hazelnut oil and raspberry vinaigrette, and you have a typical Pacific Northwest entrée.

6 medium red tomatoes

Salt, to taste

3 tablespoons extra virgin olive oil

3 ears corn, kernels removed from the cob

1 tablespoon finely chopped shallots

1 teaspoon finely chopped garlic

1 teaspoon chopped fresh oregano

2 tablespoon white wine vinegar

3 dashes Tabasco sauce

1 teaspoon coarse salt

½ teaspoon freshly ground black pepper

½ red bell pepper, cored, seeded, and diced

½ yellow bell pepper, cored, seeded, and diced

1 tablespoon chopped fresh Italian flat-leaf parsley

1 tablespoon chopped fresh basil plus 6 sprigs
    for garnish

¼ cup grated Asiago cheese

¼ cup coarse toasted bread crumbs

1 pound fresh Dungeness crabmeat, picked clean
    of shell and cartilage

Edible flowers for garnish

Slice the tops off of the tomatoes and reserve them for garnish. Slice about ⅛ inch off the bottoms of the tomatoes, so they stand upright. Hollow out the tomatoes, saving the pulp and liquid. Lightly salt the tomato cavities and invert on paper towels, to drain excess moisture. Mash the pulp and liquid through a strainer and discard the seeds. Set this tomato purée aside.

Heat 1 tablespoon of the olive oil in a medium sauté pan over a medium-high heat. Sauté the corn, shallots, garlic, and oregano for 2 to 3 minutes, or until tender. Set aside to cool.

In a small bowl, whisk together the reserved tomato purée, the remaining 2 tablespoons olive oil, vinegar, Tabasco, coarse salt, and black pepper. Set this vinaigrette aside.

In a large bowl, gently toss together the reserved corn mixture with the red and yellow bell pepper, parsley, basil, cheese, bread crumbs, Dungeness crab, and the reserved vinaigrette. Be careful not to break up the lumps of crabmeat—toss until just combined.

Stuff the tomatoes with the crab mixture. Garnish with basil sprigs, edible flowers, and the tomato tops, set slightly askew.

from Michael Kimmel, Tarpy's Roadhouse, Monterey, California

Swiss Tomato Fondue

Serves 6 to 8

**Who says that fondue is a thing of the past?
Dig out your fondue pot—you're going to need
it for this distinctive Swiss Tomato Fondue. In
this fondue pot you will find the traditional
nutty-mellow flavors of Gruyère and
Emmentaler cheeses with the added fillip of
sweet tomato juice and chopped tomatoes.**

8 to 10 plum tomatoes (about 1 pound),
    peeled, seeded, and chopped
2 cloves garlic, finely minced
½ cup tomato juice
10 ounces Gruyère cheese, grated
10 ounces Emmentaler cheese, grated
4 teaspoons cornstarch
1 tablespoon heavy cream
Freshly ground white pepper
Generous pinch dried oregano

Combine the tomatoes and garlic in a fondue pot
over a medium heat on a stovetop. Stirring
continuously, cook until soft, about 4 to 5 minutes.
Add ¼ cup of the tomato juice and cook until very
hot, about 3 to 4 minutes. Add the Gruyère and
Emmentaler cheeses.

Mix the cornstarch with the remaining ¼ cup of
tomato juice and the cream until smooth. Stir into

the tomato-cheese mixture and continue to cook and stir until the cheese is melted. Season with the white pepper and oregano and transfer the pot to the fondue base over a low flame.

Note: You may serve the Swiss Tomato Fondue with a crusty country bread, cut in 1-inch cubes, or small pieces of ham or mixed sausages, or even blanched vegetables, such as asparagus or broccoli.

from André Lengacher, Lugano Swiss Bistro, Carmel, California

Fresh Fennel and Tomato Bake

Serves 4 to 6

Although it stands on its own as a wonderful vegetarian side, try serving this delicate but satisfying dish as a base for any highly flavored roasted poultry—like duck, game hens, or even a robust roasting chicken. Just place the finished roast right on top of the baked fennel dish (which will soak up all the roast's drippings) and serve.

3 fresh fennel bulbs
    (trimmed weight about 1¼ pounds)
¼ cup extra virgin olive oil
2 cloves garlic, finely chopped
2 cups peeled, seeded, and chopped tomatoes
    (about 1 pound)
Salt and freshly ground black pepper, to taste
4 slices country-style bread, cut in ½-inch cubes
    (about 3½ to 4 cups)
¼ cup melted butter
⅓ cup grated Parmesan

Preheat the oven to 350°.

Trim the fennel bulbs by cutting off the tops, leaving about ½ inch above the bulbs and cutting away any brown spots. Cut the bulbs in half lengthwise, and then in ¼-inch-thick slices. Remove any hard central cores.

In a large sauté pan, heat the olive oil over a medium-high heat. Add the fennel slices and garlic. Sauté, turning occasionally, until just tender, 5 to 7 minutes. Add the tomatoes and season with salt and pepper. Sauté 2 to 3 minutes more. Spoon the fennel mixture, including its liquid, into a shallow baking dish, about 8 by 13 by 2 inches.

In a small bowl, toss the bread, melted butter, and Parmesan. Place the bread cubes evenly over the fennel mixture. Bake until golden brown and bubbling, about 20 to 25 minutes. Serve warm.

from Susan Ardell, Carmel, California

Fuzzy Bomb

Mother's Tomato Bread Pudding

Serves 4 to 6

There have been baked tomato pudding recipes around since pre–Civil War days. It's a firmly rooted traditional dish on most dining tables of the South. Tomato bread pudding is a warming sweet-tart melange, a welcome addition to any dinner, be it festive or everyday. Here is the genre at its most tried and true, tested on generations of grateful tomato lovers.

2 cups peeled and seeded (about 1 pound),
    or 1 (16-ounce) can tomato pieces in juice
3 slices country-style bread,
    cut in ½-inch cubes (about 3 cups)
1 cup golden brown sugar
¾ cup water
1 teaspoon salt
½ cup (4 ounces) softened butter
2 teaspoons freshly squeezed lemon juice

Preheat the oven to 375°. Cut the tomatoes in small pieces, reserving all juice. Toast the bread cubes lightly. (Day-old bread is fine.) Set aside.

Place the brown sugar, water, and salt in a medium saucepan over a low heat. Cook until the sugar and water have combined, about 5 minutes. Add the tomatoes, bread cubes, butter, and lemon juice. Cook, stirring very gently until the butter has melted, 3 to 4 minutes. Pour the tomato mixture into a casserole or baking dish. Bake until bubbling, 30 to 35 minutes. Serve piping hot.

from Joan Nielsen's mother, Helen Nielsen Allen

Ceylon

Vegetable-Stuffed Tomatoes with White Bean Vinaigrette

Serves 8

These baked stuffed tomatoes are superb whether served at room temperature or chilled. They are filled with delicate squash (with a hint of lemon marmalade), artichokes, and sweet Hungarian peppers and bound by goat cheese and herbs. They are surrounded by sublime white beans in a extra virgin olive oil and sherry wine vinaigrette.

3 tablespoons extra virgin olive oil

½ red onion, chopped

1½ cups chopped summer squash,
    such as zucchini, sunburst, or patty pan

3 tablespoon lemon marmalade

1½ cups chopped cooked artichoke hearts

1 large sweet Hungarian pepper, roasted,
    peeled, seeded, and chopped (about ½ cup)

8 ounces goat cheese, crumbled

1 tablespoon fresh thyme leaves

¼ cup coarsely chopped basil

Salt and freshly ground black pepper, to taste

8 medium tomatoes, preferably bell pepper
    tomatoes or stuffer tomatoes,
    which are hollow inside

1 cup fresh bread crumbs

White Bean Vinaigrette (recipe follows)

*"Bacon" made from colored pasta
is used here for decoration.*

Heat 1 tablespoon of the olive oil in a medium sauté
pan over a medium-low heat. Add the onion and
sauté for 3 to 5 minutes, or until transparent. Add
the squash and lemon marmalade and sauté for 2 to
3 minutes, or until the squash is still crispy tender.
Remove from the heat and add the artichoke hearts,
sweet pepper, goat cheese, thyme, and basil. Mix
well and season with salt and black pepper.

Preheat the oven to 400°. Slice the tops off of the
tomatoes. Slice about ⅛-inch off the bottoms of
tomatoes, so they stand upright. If not using
stuffer-type tomatoes, hollow out firm red tomatoes
and discard excess pulp and seeds. Stuff with the
vegetable mixture. Sprinkle with the bread crumbs
and drizzle with the remaining 2 tablespoons of
olive oil. Bake for 15 minutes. Set aside to cool.
When ready to serve, place the stuffed tomatoes
on a platter, or on individual plates, and surround
them with the White Bean Vinaigrette.

White Bean Vinaigrette

1½ cups great northern white beans,
    soaked in water overnight

2 cups chicken stock or water

3 sprigs thyme

1 small carrot, chopped in 2 or 3 pieces

1 small onion, halved

1½ cups red cherry tomatoes

4 shallots, finely chopped

¼ cup sherry wine vinegar

¾ cup extra virgin olive oil

¼ cup chopped fresh parsley

¼ cup chopped fresh basil

Salt and freshly ground black pepper, to taste

Simmer the beans, chicken stock, carrots, onions, and thyme in a medium saucepan for about 1½ hours, or until the beans are tender. (Add more liquid if the beans are not completely covered while cooking.) Drain the beans, reserving some of the liquid, and discard the thyme sprigs, carrot, and onion. Cool the beans.

Place the beans in a medium bowl and add ¼ cup of the reserved bean liquid, the cherry tomatoes, shallots, vinegar, olive oil, parsley, and basil. Season with salt and pepper.

from Cal Stamenov, executive chef, Highlands Inn, Carmel, California

Green Tomato and Apple Pie

Makes 1 9-inch pie, serving 6 to 8

When your family and friends taste this deliciously sweet pie for the first time, without knowing what its ingredients are, they'll be amazed!

Pie dough (recipe follows)

3 cups green (unripe) tomatoes,
    cut in ⅛-inch-thick slices

2 cups peeled, cored, ⅛-inch-thick slices of tart
    green apples, such as Pippin or Granny Smith

1 tablespoon freshly squeezed lemon juice

1¼ cup sugar

¼ teaspoon salt

5 tablespoons all-purpose flour

½ teaspoon nutmeg

½ teaspoon cinnamon

⅛ teaspoon powdered ginger

1 tablespoon minced lemon zest

¼ cup butter (4 ounces), cut in small bits

¼ cup gold raisins

Begin by making the pie dough and rolling out the bottom crust to fit a 9-inch pie pan. Cover this crust and the dough for the top crust with a kitchen towel so they won't dry out.

Preheat the oven to 425°. Place the tomatoes on paper towels to dry. In a medium bowl, toss the apple slices with the lemon juice. Add the tomatoes and toss gently.

In a small bowl, combine the sugar, salt, flour, nutmeg, cinnamon, ginger, and lemon zest. Carefully fold this spice mixture into the tomato and apple mixture. Spoon this pie filling into the pie shell and dot with the butter and raisins. Roll out the remaining pie dough and cover the top of the pie with it. Trim the dough evenly, tuck the top edge under the bottom edge, and crimp them together decoratively with your fingers or the tines of a fork. Slit the top crust in several places to make vents for the steam to escape and brush with the egg wash.

Bake the pie in the center of the oven for 15 minutes. Lower the oven heat to 325° and bake for about 50 minutes more, or until the crust is golden brown. Check to see if the pie drips during baking and, if it does, put a piece of aluminum foil under the pie to catch the drippings.

Pie Dough

2½ cups all-purpose flour

1 cup cold salted butter, (8 ounces)
  cut into ½-inch cubes

¼ to ½ cup ice cold water

1 egg, whisked well with 2 tablespoons milk
  (for egg wash)

Place 4 ice cubes in a 1-cup measure and fill with water. Set aside. Place the flour into the bowl of a food processor fitted with a metal blade. Add the butter cubes and hand mix them around in the flour to coat them. Pulse the processor several times until the butter is the size of peas.

Remove the ice cubes from the water and pour off all but ½ cup. While pulsing, pour the ice water into the processor through the feed tube. Stop when the mixture just begins to come together.

It should look a little dry and crumbly. (When the weather is damp or rainy, you will need much less water than on a sunny, dry day. Try using less water at first, as you can always add more, if needed.)

Place the dough on a lightly floured surface and gently push it together with your hands. Divide it into 2 pieces, one slightly larger than the other, and gently shape them into flat discs. The dough can be worked now or refrigerated for up to 4 days. It is best rolled out either at room temperature or after it has rested, out of the refrigerator, for ten minutes. It can also be frozen, well wrapped, for up to 4 weeks.

Pie from Gary Ibsen; Pie Dough from Gayle Ortiz, of Gayle's Bakery, Capitola, California

Cherokee Chocolate

Tomato Granité

Makes about 1 quart

You can use this terrific icy tomato treat in a
myriad of creative ways: as a refreshing cooler
in the middle of a hot day, as a palate cleanser
between the courses of a heavy meal, or on top
of a salad of wild baby greens (it will melt over
the greens as you eat). Best yet, freeze it solid
flat, break it up into shards of tomato ice, and
use these jagged pieces to decorate a shrimp
cocktail—or even a Bloody Mary. This Tomato
Granité is made with freshly chopped dill, but
you could use chives, Italian flat-leaf parsley,
basil, or even mint.

¾ cup water

⅓ cup sugar

1 envelope gelatin, softened in ¼ cup cold water

1½ pounds ripe red tomatoes, peeled, seeded,
    and chopped (about 3 cups)

2 tablespoons freshly squeezed lemon juice

1 tablespoon finely chopped fresh dill

Pinch of salt

Heat the water and sugar in a small saucepan over
a low heat. Cook for about 5 minutes, stirring until
the sugar is dissolved. Stir in the softened gelatin
until it is dissolved. Remove from the heat and set
aside to cool completely.

Pass the tomatoes through a food mill fitted with a medium disk. Or push the tomatoes through a medium strainer with a wooden spoon. Add this tomato purée to the sugar water, stirring until well blended. Stir in the lemon juice, dill, and the pinch of salt.

Pour the tomato mixture into a metal bowl. Place the bowl in the freezer. Freeze until the granité gets hard around the edges, in about 30 minutes, and mix the frozen part in with the rest. Do this every 30 minutes, for about 3 hours, or until consistently frozen through. Pack into a container, seal, and keep in the freezer for no more than 2 days. Alternatively, you may freeze the granité in a 9 by 13 by 2-inch metal pan until solid. When ready for use, break up into shards of tomato ice.

from Joan Nielsen

Anna Russian

Yellow Tomato Flans with Parmesan Wafers

Makes 10 to 12 flans

An absolutely heavenly custard, with the elusive elegant flavor note of fresh tomato and the scent of citrus and basil, this dessert is an heirloom in itself. The added treat of a crisp Parmesan wafer is icing on the cake.

1 pound yellow tomatoes, peeled, seeded,
    and chopped (about 2 cups)
½ cup sugar
1 teaspoon grated orange zest
3 tablespoons finely chopped fresh basil leaves
Salt and freshly ground black pepper, to taste
1 quart heavy cream
15 egg yolks
2 cups grated Parmesan cheese
Basil leaves for garnish

Pass the tomatoes through a food mill fitted with a fine disk. Or, push the tomatoes through a fine strainer with a wooden spoon. Cook this tomato purée, sugar, orange zest, and basil in a dry, non-stick pan over a medium-low heat until most of the moisture has evaporated and the purée is the consistency of a thin paste. Take care not to scorch. Season with salt and pepper.

Simmer the cream in a medium saucepan over a low heat. Stir in the tomato purée mixture and blend well. Simmer for 5 to 7 minutes.

Preheat the oven to 300°.

Place the egg yolks in a medium bowl. Beat with an electric mixer for 3 to 5 minutes, or until a light lemon color. While still beating, slowly add 1 cup of the hot cream mixture to the yolks. Blend in the rest of the cream until smooth. Season with a little salt and pepper. Strain this mixture and pour into 10 to 12 small ramekins. Place the ramekins in a large shallow baking pan, fill the pan with boiling water to reach ⅓ of the way up the sides of the ramekins, and bake for 40 to 45 minutes or until set. Remove the ramekins from the water bath to cool.

Place the Parmesan cheese in a layer about ¾-inch thick on a parchment-lined baking sheet. Bake for 1 to 1½ hours in a 225° oven, or until crisp. Cool and break into 2-inch wafers. Serve the tomato flans chilled or at room temperature and garnish each with a Parmesan wafer and leaves of fresh basil.

from Jim Gallivan, Fess Parker's Wine Country Inn, Los Olivos, California

Mandarin Cross

Grandmother Miller's Homemade Tomato Juice

Makes about 20 quarts

This is a recipe for a grand, old-fashioned tomato juice straight from a third-generation Midwesterner in one of the tomato-growing capitals of the U.S.—Indiana. It is usually prepared with at least a bushel of tomatoes, but you may reduce that to a manageable half of a bushel! Go ahead and increase the amount of tomatoes as your expertise and desires dictate. You'll never regret the labor of making this juice, for the incredible payoff is enjoyed throughout the year. As Grandmother Miller used to say, "Listen to the tomatoes, they'll tell you what to do."

1 bushel ripe red tomatoes (equivalent to
    4 pecks or 32 quarts, dry weight)
2 tablespoons salt
2 jars pickling spices (about 2 ounces each),
    tied securely into 2 bundles in several layers
    of cheesecloth

Begin slicing off and discarding the top quarter (the stem end) of the tomatoes, putting the tomatoes into two 20-quart stockpots as you go along.

Slowly bring the tomatoes to a boil over a low heat. (Don't rush this, because you do not want to scorch the bottom layers of the tomatoes.) Keep moving the tomatoes around with a wooden spoon while you add more of them. When all the tomatoes are in the pots and beginning to boil, add 1 tablespoon salt and 1 bundle of pickling spices to each pot. Now bring to a full rolling boil. Once at a rolling boil turn off the heat and remove, but don't discard the spice bag.

Pass the tomatoes through a food mill fitted with a fine disk, or a juicer that removes the skins and seeds. Or, force through a strainer with a wooden spoon. Return the tomato juice and the spice bags to the cleaned stockpots. Bring to a second boil and then lower the heat to a simmer. Watching carefully, cook for 10 to 15 minutes, depending on the tomatoes (see notes below). Remove and discard the spice bags.

Pour the juice into 20 sterilized quart jars, leaving about ¼-inch headroom. Wipe the rims clean, and screw on the lids. (Don't screw the lids down too tight.) Place the jars in boiling water to cover, and process for 45 minutes. Remove from the water and cool down overnight. Store in a cool dark place for up to a year.

Note: Purchase "canning tomatoes" from a grower or farmers' market, late in the growing season. They are not very pretty, maybe blemished, maybe a tad too ripe, but definitely less expensive. They are almost always sweet and desirable for making juice.

Go light on the salt. If you oversalt, there's no saving the end result. You can always add salt and freshly ground black pepper to your taste after the juice is made.

You are at the mercy of the tomatoes you use. If they are watery, they'll need boiling down a little longer. If they are firmer, they'll need less cooking time. Learn to listen to the tomatoes, you'll get the hang of it —and they really will tell you what to do.

This is an all-day affair. Enlist the help of family or friends and have a good time making this unforgettable homemade juice. Who knows, it may become your yearly ritual.

from Joan Nielsen, via her Indiana relative, Bob Miller

Tigerella

Classic Tomato Sauce with Fresh Tomatoes

Makes about 3 cups, serving 4 as a sauce for pasta

This is a simple, easy-to-prepare fresh tomato sauce that will become a kitchen staple. Its flavor isn't overwhelming, but rather a base note to expand upon wherever tomato sauce is called for. You may leave it chunky or blend it smooth. Either way it is just plain wonderful!

2 tablespoons extra virgin olive oil
1 small onion, chopped
1 clove garlic, minced (optional)
1½ pounds ripe red tomatoes, peeled, seeded, hard cores removed, and chopped (about 3 cups)
Salt and freshly ground pepper, to taste

Warm the olive oil in a small saucepan over a medium heat. Add the onions and garlic and cook for about 3 minutes, or until onions are translucent. Add the tomatoes and any of their liquid. Cook for 7 to 10 minutes. (The cooking time may vary according to the ripeness, variety of tomato used, or quality of the tomatoes, and will dictate how long you cook the sauce. Use your best judgment.) Season with the salt and pepper. Leave chunky or blend in a food processor fitted with a metal blade.

from Joan Nielsen

Three Tomato Salsas

These salsa recipes were created especially for heirloom tomatoes. The green salsa has the zing of lime juice, cilantro, and green onions; the gold is succulent with sweet mango, mint, and orange juice; and the red is a classic variation with red bell pepper, red onion, and basil. Each has the wonderful kick of jalapeños and garlic, which you may want to boost or cut back on.

Green Tomato Salsa

1 pound green tomatoes, cut in ¼-inch dice

2 cloves garlic, minced

4 green onions, including white and green parts, thinly sliced

⅓ cup finely chopped cilantro

1½ tablespoons freshly squeezed lime juice

1 jalapeño pepper, stemmed, seeded, and minced

Coarse salt and freshly ground pepper, to taste

Mix all of the above ingredients and refrigerate for at least an hour to blend the flavors together. Serve in a festive bowl surrounded with warmed and salted tortilla chips. Makes about 2½ cups.

Gold Tomato Salsa

1 pound gold tomatoes, cut in ¼-inch dice

2 tablespoons golden bell pepper,
   cut in ¼-inch dice

⅓ cup mango, cut in ¼-inch dice

1½ jalapeño peppers, stemmed,
   seeded, and minced

2 tablespoons freshly squeezed orange juice

2 tablespoons finely chopped mint

Coarse salt and freshly ground pepper, to taste

Mix all of the above ingredients and refrigerate
for at least an hour to blend the flavors together.
Serve in a festive bowl surrounded with warmed
and salted tortilla chips. Makes about 2½ cups.

Red Tomato Salsa

1 pound red tomatoes, cut in ¼-inch dice

½ red onion, cut in ¼-inch dice

1½ tablespoons red bell pepper, cut in
   ¼-inch dice

2 cloves garlic, minced

1½ tablespoons freshly squeezed lemon juice

1 jalapeño pepper, stemmed, seeded, and minced

2 tablespoon finely chopped basil

Coarse salt and freshly ground pepper, to taste

Mix all of the above ingredients and refrigerate
for at least an hour to blend the flavors together.
Serve in a festive bowl surrounded with warmed
and salted tortilla chips. Makes about 2¾ cups.

**from Bunyan B. Fortune Jr., executive chef,
La Playa Hotel, Carmel-by-the-Sea, California**

Vine-Ripe Golden Tomato Marmalade

Makes about 7 cups

This luscious golden marmalade is a superb accompaniment to any main course, from lamb chops to fried chicken to roast pork. Or if you wish, serve it alongside homemade corn bread for a great addition to any dinner menu. You may vary the type of tomato, as your garden dictates, and the results will be equally delicious. This is not a heavily sugared marmalade and needs to be refrigerated to maintain its freshness.

6 pounds ripe yellow tomatoes
1 pound sugar
2 cinnamon sticks
1 star anise
3 cloves

With a sharp knife, score the skin of the tomatoes in an X on the blossom end. Place in boiling water for 15 to 20 seconds. (This may be done in batches.) Plunge the tomatoes into a large bowl of iced water to stop the cooking process. Slip the peel off and remove any hard cores. Cut in half and squeeze out the seeds.

In a deep pot, combine the peeled tomatoes with the sugar, cinnamon, star anise, and cloves. Bring to a rolling boil, then lower the heat to a simmer and cook for 1½ to 2 hours, or until the tomatoes are falling apart and beginning to thicken. (This may take more time, depending upon the water content of the tomatoes.) Watch carefully to avoid scorching and stir often. Remove from heat when consistency is similar to a thick jam. Discard the cinnamon, star anise, and cloves. Store in airtight jars, refrigerated, for 2 to 3 weeks.

from James Waller, executive chef, Duck Club Restaurant, Monterey, California

Resources

Seed Sources

The seed sources listed below meet my criteria for suppliers of heirloom tomatoes.

ARCHIAS' SEED STORE

106 East Main St.
Sedalia, MO 65301-3849
(816) 826-1330
Seeds: Tomatoes, open-pollinated vegetables, flowers, herbs, and bee supplies. One of the oldest seed houses in U.S.

COOKS GARDEN

P.O. Box 535
Londonderry, VT 05148
(802) 824-3400
(802) 824-3027 (fax)
Seeds: Favorite varieties of tomatoes and annual and perennial herbs.

GLECKLER'S SEEDMEN

Metamora, OH 43540
(419) 644-2211
Fantastic collection of tomato and vegetable seeds from around the world.

GRANDVIEW FARMS

12942 Dupont Rd.
Sebastopol, CA 95472
dawson@sonic.net
Seeds: Many hard-to-find heirloom tomatoes.

HEIRLOOM SEEDS

P.O. Box 245
West Elizabeth, PA 15088

JOHNNY'S SELECTED SEEDS

310 Foss Hill Rd.
Albion, Maine 04910
(207) 437-4301
Seeds: Heirloom tomatoes, vegetables, flowers, and grains. Garden supplies.

photo on page 138: *Paul Robeson*

LITTLE RIVER GARDEN SEEDS

P.O. Box W-1
Carmel, CA 93921
(831) 625-2818 (fax)
food4you@redshift.com
Seeds: Heirloom tomatoes.

SEEDS BLUM

Idaho City Stage
Boise, ID 83706
(208) 342-0858
Seeds: Tomatoes and great selection of potatoes.

SEEDS OF CHANGE

P.O. Box 15700
Santa Fe, NM 87596-5700
(888) 762-7333 www.seedsofchange.com
Seeds: Certified organic tomatoes, vegetables, flowers, herbs, and grains. Garden supplies.

SEED SAVERS EXCHANGE

3076 N. Winn Rd.
Decorah, IA 52101
(319) 382-5990
(319) 382-5872 (fax)
Seeds: Tomatoes, vegetables, and flowers. Garden supplies and books.

SHEPHERD'S GARDEN SEEDS

30 Irene Street
Torrington, CT 06790-6658
(860) 482-0532
(860) 482-0532 (fax)
Seeds: Tomatoes, flowers, and vegetables (great selection). Garden supplies.

SOUTHERN EXPOSURE SEED EXCHANGE

P.O. Box 170
Earlysville, VA 22936
(804) 973-4703
(804) 973-8717 (fax)
Seeds: Tomatoes and great selection of open-pollinated vegetables, flowers, and herbs.

TERRITORIAL SEED COMPANY
P.O. Box 157
Cottage Grove, OR 97424-0061
(541) 942-9547
Seeds: Tomatoes and great selection of open-pollinated vegetables, specializing in early-season (cool-summer) varieties.

TOMATO GROWERS SUPPLY CO.
P.O. Box 2237
Fort Meyers, Fl 33902
(941) 768-1119
Seeds: Tomatoes and peppers. Garden supplies and books.

TOTALLY TOMATOES
P.O. Box 1626
Augusta, GA 30903-1626
(706) 663-9772 (fax)
Seeds: Tomatoes and peppers. Garden supplies.

Garden Suppliers

CHARLEY'S GREENHOUSE SUPPLY
1569 Memorial Highway
Mount Vernon, WA 98273-9721
(800) 322-4707
(800) 233-3078 (fax)

GARDENER'S SUPPLY COMPANY
128 Intervale Rd.
Burlington, VT 05401
(800) 315-4005
Greenhouse and irrigation equipment.

GARDENS ALIVE!
5100 Schenley Pl.
Lawrenceburg, IN 47025
(812) 537-8650

HOME CANNING SUPPLY & SPECIALTIES
2017 La Brea St.
Ramona, CA 92065
(619) 788-0520
(619) 789-4745 (fax)
Home canning supplies.

PEACEFUL VALLEY FARM SUPPLY
P.O. Box 2209
Grass Valley, CA 95945
(530) 272-4769
(888) 784-1722
Organic fertilizers, natural pest management, growing supplies, irrigation supplies, cover crop seeds, and garden tools.

SEASON EXTENDERS
P.O. Box 312
Stratford, CT 06497
(203) 375-1317
Greenhouse supplies.

Tomato Organizations

CALIFORNIA TOMATO COMMISSION
1625 E. Shaw Ave.
Fresno, CA 93710
(209) 230-0116

FLORIDA TOMATO COMMITTEE
P.O. Box 140635
Orlando, FL 32814
(407) 894-3071

THE HEIRLOOM SEED PROJECT
The Landis Valley Museum
2451 Kissel Hill Rd.
Lancaster, PA 17601
(717) 569-0401

SEED SAVERS EXCHANGE
3076 N. Winn Rd.
Decorah, IA 52101
(319) 382-5990
(319) 382-5872 (fax)

THE TOMATO GENETICS RESOURCE CENTER
Genetic Resources Conservation Program
University of California at Davis
Davis, CA 95616
(813) 768-1119

Tomato Festivals

BRADLEY COUNTY PINK TOMATO FESTIVAL
Chamber of Commerce
104 N. Myrtle
Warren, AR 71671
(501) 226-5225
Second weekend in June

GREAT TOMATO FESTIVAL
Flickertail Gardens-Fairgrounds
#9 Parkway
Minot, ND 58701
(701) 838-4429
Mid-August

THOMAS JEFFERSON'S TOMATOE FAIRE
The Community Market
Main at 12th St.
Lynchburg, VA 24504
(804) 847-1499
First weekend in August

LA TOMATINA
Buñol, Spain
For information:
http://www.cyberspain.com/life/tomatina.htm
*Last Wednesday of August, between 11:00 A.M.
and 1:00 P.M.*

    *This is an all-out tomato-throwing party! Yes, it is
true. Since 1944, people dressed in traditional white have*

come to this little town thirty miles west of Valencia, just to sling ripe tomatoes. There is a week-long festival with music, fireworks, and food as well. A tip from those who've been—bring a pair of swim goggles!

TOMATOFESTˢᴹ
P.O. Box W-1
Carmel, CA 93921
food4you@redshift.com
(831) 625-2818 (fax)
Sunday in late August or early September

Additional Reading

Ashworth, Suzanne. *Seed to Seed*.
   Decorah, IA: Seed Saver Publications, 1991.

Bennett, Jennifer. *The Tomato Handbook*.
   Buffalo, NY: Firefly Books, 1997.

Campbell, Stu. *Let It Rot: The Gardener's Guide to Composting*. Pownal, VT: Storey
   Communications, 1990.

Cool, Jesse. *Tomatoes: A Country Garden Cookbook*.
   San Francisco: Collins Publishers, 1994.

Cutter, Karan Davis, ed. *Tantalizing Tomatoes*.
   Brooklyn Botanic Garden Publications. Hand-
   books in the 21st-Century Series, #150, 1997.

Doty, Walter L. And A. Cort Sinnes. *All About Tomatoes*. San Francisco: Ortho Books, 1981.

Jordon, Michele Anna. *The Good Cook's Book of Tomatoes*. New York: Addison-Wesley, 1995.

Luebbermann, Mimi. *Terrific Tomatoes*.
   San Francisco, Chronicle Books, 1994.

Riotte, Louise. *Carrots Love Tomatoes: Secrets of Companion Planting for Successful Gardening*.
   Pownal, VT: Storey Communications, 1998.

Smith, Andrew. *The Tomato in America: Early History, Culture, and Cookery.* Columbia, South Carolina: University of South Carolina Press, 1994.

The Internet

Web sites come and go, so with that in mind, here's an offering of current sites for accessing tomato data.

The Official Home Page for California
Fresh Market Tomatoes
http://www.tomato.org/

Purdue University Horticultural Dept.
http://www.hort.purdue.edu - Hort 410 Tomatoes

Prevention Magazine's Healthy Ideas
http://www.healthyideas.com/cooking/news/980409.
news.html

Ohio State University extension
http://www.ag.ohio-state.edu/~ohioline/
hyg-fact/1000/1645.html

University of California at Davis Commercial
Processing of Tomatoes
http://vric.ucdavis.edu/vrichome/html/
selectnewcrop.tomproc.htm

Purple Tomatillo

Gary Ibsen

Few people can turn their passion for food and wine into a profession as successfully as Gary Ibsen has done. In the early seventies, Gary published a series of regional food, wine, and restaurant magazines then joined, respectively, the wine divisions of The Coca-Cola Company and Seagrams for several years as marketing director. His love of cooking led him to study with Marcella Hazan in Italy and regional cooking styles throughout North America, open a popular Cajun/Creole restaurant in Carmel, California, win a March of Dimes cooking award with actor/director Clint Eastwood, and cook for the television audience on *Good Morning America* with Joan Lunden. Gary served on the national board of directors of the American Institute of Wine & Food with Julia Child, and co-founded the Monterey Bay Chapter of A.I.W.F. He has given talks about tomatoes for the University of California, local garden clubs, and the Culinary Historians of Southern California, and has made several appearances on P. Allen Smith's nationally syndicated television show, *Gardens*. Gary was founder, publisher, and editorial director of the award-winning *Adventures In Dining* magazine.

Gary's passion for growing organic tomatoes led to developing the TomatoFest and a gardening program for elementary schools. In 1998, Gary's seventh annual TomatoFest was a sold-out charity event that received national media attention. To contact Gary: P. O. Box W-1, Carmel, CA 93921; e-mail: food4 you@redshift.com; Internet: www.tomatofest.com.

Joan Nielsen

With an education in fine arts and formal training as a graphic designer, Joan Nielsen was an art director before her passion for food led her to professional cooking, recipe development, and food writing. Here, her preparation was no less thorough, having studied with Julia Child, Wolfgang Puck, and Diana Kennedy. Before embarking on *The Great Tomato Book*, Nielsen edited cookbooks, developed and tested recipes, and wrote and food-styled nearly one hundred shows for cable and network television. She has worked with such luminaries as Jacques Pepin, Joachim Splichal, Hans Röckenwagner, and Julie Sahni. She is currently the editor of the *Food Journal* of the Culinary Historians of Southern California.